KT-381-825

MESSAGE AND MEDIUM:
A Course in Critical Reading

77

Lionel Jackson
Moray House College of Education
Edinburgh

Mary Jackson
Scottish Centre for Education Overseas
Moray House College of Education
Edinburgh

St. Columba's High School,
Dunfermline.

HODDER AND STOUGHTON
LONDON SYDNEY AUCKLAND TORONTO

To the many colleagues and students who have helped us by reading, discussing and commenting on much of the material in this book.

British Library Cataloguing in Publication Data

Message and medium.
1. Readers – 1950-
I. Jackson, Lionel   II. Jackson, Mary
428.6   PE1120

ISBN   0 340 26903 0

First published 1981
Copyright © 1981 H. L. and M. G. Jackson

All rights reserved. No part of this publication
may be reproduced or transmitted in any form or
by any means, electronic or mechanical, including
photocopy, recording or any information storage and retrieval
system, without permission in writing from the publisher.
Printed in Great Britain for Hodder and Stoughton
Educational, a division of Hodder and Stoughton Ltd,
Mill Road, Dunton Green, Sevenoaks, Kent
by Richard Clay (The Chaucer Press) Ltd., Bungay, Suffolk.

Contents

1. Staying Alive   (Peter Laurie)   1
2. Horse Sense   (Anonymous)   6
3. John, Me and the Lancashire Treasure
   (Ray Connolly)   9
4. Breeding Out Faults   (Gerald Leach)   13
5. The Looking Glass Kids   (David Lewis)   16
6. Rebel Daughter   (Mary Kenny)   20
7. The Tribe That Has Lost its Way   (Jill Tweedie)   24
8. Childhood Discipline   (Margaret Mead)   28
9. Pop   (Tony Jasper)   32
10. Child's Play   (Willis Hall)   35
11. The Occupational Culture of the Boxer   (S. K. Weinberg and H. Arond)   41
12. Life Really Starts When I Press That Button
   (Alistair MacLean)   46
13. Seaside Holiday   (Anthony Hern)   51
14. Life in the Year AD 2000   (Colin Leicester)   54
15. Notes on a War   (Kenneth Allsop)   58
16. Supernature   (Lyall Watson)   61
17. Happiness   (Malcom Muggeridge)   67
18. Seconds Out   (Michael Osborne)   70
19. The Function of the Dream   (J. A. Hadfield)   74
20. Their Time is Nearly Run Out   (Ruth Harrison)   78
21. Fox-hunting Debate   (various authors)   82
22. Courting Customs   (E. S. Turner)   90
23. The Sexes are Really Different   (Benjamin Spock)   95
24. The Great Male Plot   (Casey Miller and Kate Swift)   100
25. A Race of Thinking Animals?   (Edwin Muir)   105
26. Death Wish Without Pride   (Geoffrey Robertson)   108
27. Euthanasia   (F. R. Barry)   112
28. Changes in Working Class Life   (Richard Hoggart)   117
29. See Big Plane   (Frank Smith)   121

30. An Enormous Achievement   (Walter Nash)   126
31. Incidental Gestures   (Desmond Morris)   133
32. Summerhill Education Vs Standard Education
    (A. S. Neill)   136
33. Scripts People Live   (Claude M. Steiner and Hogie
    Wyckoff)   142
34. The Trouble with People   (Vance Packard)   148
35. Package Tour   (Sue Arnold)   154
36. Paradise   (Laurie Lee)   158

Glossary   164

Acknowledgements   170

1 Staying Alive

Peter Laurie

Peter Laurie was born in Reigate in 1937 and was educated at Lancing. After reading mathematics and law at Christ's College, Cambridge, he worked as a writer and photographer for Vogue, did freelance writing for the Daily Mail and the Sunday Telegraph, and joined the Sunday Times Magazine shortly after it started in 1965. From 1974 to 1978 he contributed a satirical column, 'Pig Ignorant', to New Scientist. He is now editor of the magazine Practical Computing. Peter Laurie lives in London.

========

1 In a 100 years, our great grandchildren will find it appalling to imagine the river of death that runs outside our doors today. They will wonder how we could tolerate it. How *can* we tolerate it? Only because we're so used to cars that we don't notice them. But just imagine that instead of the highway, we had a high tension wire 5 along the outside edge of every pavement, charged with enough electricity so that the least contact could kill. Would we carelessly let our children run to the shop on the corner for a packet of sweets, saying 'Step carefully over the wire, dear'?

2 In a 100 years' time the untamed car at our doors will seem as 10 horrible as eighteenth-century operations without anaesthetics do to us now.

3 At first the car seemed a good idea. Now it is a lethal tyrant. As Dr Mackay, of the Road Accident Research Unit at Birmingham University, points out, there are 'some 130,000 fatalities and perhaps 15 1,700,000 serious casualties in the western world *every* year. These figures are on the scale of a medium-sized war continuing all the time.' In Britain, the car at this moment kills four times as many people a year as the Luftwaffe did during the war years.

4 The car is dangerous because it is badly conceived and badly 20 designed. Driving, considered as a task set for the computer of the brain, is just on the limit of what it can do. Driving is a great deal more demanding than flying an aeroplane, yet anyone who can read a numberplate at twenty-five yards and navigate slowly round the block is allowed to take several dozen horsepower out on the 25 road; compare that with the countless precautions that are taken to train and test aircrew and the extreme vigilance imposed on the mechanical condition of their machines.

1

5   For a device in which mistakes are so easy to make, the car is not well adapted to soften the results. Next time you get in your car, look *30* at what is in front of you. Notice the shaft of the steering wheel, aimed like a lance from the front right-hand corner of the car straight at your heart. See how the steering wheel spreads its spokes to crush your ribs flat. Check the ignition key, placed to dig under your right knee-cap and prise it off. See the driving mirror poised to flatten your *35* left eye and the parcel shelf to break your legs below the knee and the wind-screen that will wrap itself round your head and then give, clawing the flesh from your face as you dive involuntarily through it.

6   If, as is not unlikely, you at some point run into another car, or a lamp-post or a wall, at the modest speed of sixty miles per hour, the *40* effect will be as though you were dropped face down on all this armoury from a height of 120 feet. Next time you run down to the shops for a minute, think of the operation in these terms: would you instead, balance on the parapet of a twelve-storey building, ready for a slip of the foot or a puff of wind to hurl you down? Would you do it *45* twice a day? Would you get so used to it that you would stand there in wind and rain and dark with your children trustingly holding your hand?

7   Not only is it terrifying, it is absurd. Once one starts to look at the car with a critical eye, it becomes ridiculous. In appearance, all *50* modern production cars are· bulbous, soft, they billow out in meaningless curves and are tattooed over with bits of chrome and runic letters. It is the height of folly to give things that run into each other as hard and often as they do optical surface finish – a finish so delicate that even a fingernail will mark it, and the pressure of a hand *55* will deform the metal. When they are new they look and smell nice enough by their own standards, but within a month the glamour begins to fade, and within a year they are shabby. It is not surprising, since they stand out in the rain, and in our cities the rain is dilute sulphuric acid. *60*

8   Although the car makes it possible to go quickly and cheaply to wherever one wants, the saving of effort and expense is largely illusory. Although the labour of walking or riding is saved, it is replaced by the intense mental effort needed to stay alive. Looked at from the point of view of human engineering, the car expropriates a *65* large part of its driver's brain for the duration of the journey, to the exclusion of all other thought. Look at the strings of cars that leave every city every evening, each with its own engine and a thousand moving parts, and each with its own guiding intelligence. If these cars were packaged together in dozens, like the device we call a bus, or in *70* hundreds like the device we call a train, the same transportation of

bodies through space could be achieved at a fraction of the cost in both economic, mechanical and mental effort.

9   It is appalling to think of those thousands of minds all measuring, computing, deciding, the neurons flickering and flashing, the 75 culmination of millions of years of evolution desperately doing the calculations that could be performed by an eighth-rate computer. Not only are these calculations rather pointless, each brain has to do the same as all the other brains. As the stream of cars approaches a corner, each driver must do the same sums and make the same 80 decisions, one after the other, night after night, until after a decade the same calculation has been performed there a million times. And every so often one of these hard-pressed machines drops a decimal point, a mistake signalled by tearing metal and moaning flesh.

10   In terms of its effects on the individual the car is odd enough. In 85 many ways it seems to be supremely badly designed for its job. It is too expensive, too complicated, too fast; it distributes the work of guidance among too many people, controlling it poses problems of perception and calculation that are just on the edge of the brain's abilities, it uses too much space and it is far too dangerous.   90

11   In its context in society, it is little better. For many people the car has become an indispensable way of defining their personalities. They buy a tin corset for their shapeless souls: they buy 'the car with authority' or 'the motoring equivalent of the seven-year-itch'. They put panthers on their wheels and tigers in their tanks. The roads have 95 become a vast theatre where ordinary people put on these expensive, deadly costumes to play the parts of racing drivers and film stars. The soft, emotionally vulnerable, confused twentieth-century man shuts himself and his breeding unit into his personality mask which defines – among half a dozen possibilities – his economic success 100 and his view of his masculinity, and transforms his vacillating self into a hard, aggressive monster (within, of course, his own 'price and engine rating bracket').

12   Before modern man mingles with large numbers of strangers, he is careful to put on his mobile shield. Glazed in, isolated by speed, he 105 whirls uncomprehending through the world, shut off from contact with his fellows; shut off from understanding, he zooms headlong down the motorway of life. Not only is the car insensate, it lacks the more tender emotions. You seldom see a kind car. The metal centaur, modern man in his car, is as unpleasant a creature as one could imagine. Just as the 110 car pollutes the air, so it pollutes our perceptions of each other; just as the acid in its exhaust dissolves our buildings, so it dissolves society.

From *The Sunday Times*, 11 October 1970

1 a The author is clearly 'anti-car'. Say what his three main lines of argument are, and which groups of paragraphs cover these.

  b Within these three sections there are many separate arguments.

    (i) Which two are in your view the strongest?
    (ii) Which two are the weakest?
    (iii) Suggest replies to the weak ones.

2 a The extract might be described as an example of **rhetoric** – 'the art of using language so as to persuade or influence others' (*Shorter Oxford Dictionary*). Typical features of such language are:

    (i) the **metaphor**: an implied simile
    (ii) the **rhetorical question**: where the answer is unnecessary or understood
    (iii) the **analogy**: a parallel or similar case.

  Find an example of each in paragraph 1.

  b Other stylistic features of this passage are:

    (i) **irony**: suggesting a meaning different from the apparent meaning
    (ii) **opposition**: words or phrases placed in contrast
    (iii) **generalisation:** a statement of wide application
    (iv) **illustration:** an example or detail which supports a general idea
    (v) **imperative**: a 'command' addressed to the reader.

  Pair off the following with (i) – (v) above:

    A 'at first the car seemed a good idea. Now it is a lethal tyrant' *(line 13)*
    B 'look at what is in front of you' *(lines 30–31)*
    C 'the modest speed of sixty miles per hour' *(line 40)*
    D 'they billow out in meaningless curves and are tattooed over with bits of chrome and runic letters' *(lines 51–53)*
    E 'within a year they are shabby' *(line 58)*

  c Find one more example in the passage of each of the eight features listed in **2 a** and **2 b**.

  d Divide the following words into groups according to whether you:

4

(i) know the meaning for certain
(ii) are not sure but can guess it from the **context**
(iii) are quite uncertain:

'anaesthetics' *(line 11)*, 'Luftwaffe' *(line 19)*, 'vigilance' *(line 27)*, 'involuntarily' *(line 38)*, 'parapet' *(line 44)*, 'bulbous' *(line 51)*, 'runic' *(line 53)*, 'expropriates' *(line 65)*, 'neurons' *(line 75)*, 'corset' *(line 93)*, 'vacillating' *(line 101)*.

e Check the meaning of the words listed in **d** above and say which words from groups (ii) and (iii) it would be useful to have in your group (i) and why, in each case.

3 a Write a few paragraphs on Transport in Britain in

(i) 100 Years' Time
(ii) 1000 Years' Time.

b Write a persuasive piece, suitable for a Sunday supplement, in which you argue the case against something you dislike.

2 Horse Sense

(Anonymous)

1 If you have spent any part of this week-end in a Bank Holiday traffic jam; if you have taken a walk in a country lane and had to leap for your life every few yards; if your windows have been rattled by juggernauts or your rest ruined by revving engines and slamming doors then it's a near certainty that some time or other you will have 5
wished yet again that 'the damn things had never been invented.' But have you gone further and speculated what life would be like if the horseless carriage had never been evolved and we were back with – well, with the horse?

2 Everyone 'knows two things about the horse and one of them is 10
rather coarse,' so let's start straight in with the manure problem. It was getting all but insupportable in the Victorian era. To cross any main road in any major city in winter was like plunging into a Flemish farmyard. With the drying effect of the summer sun an August crossing of Piccadilly could be as distressing an experience as 15
a sand storm in the Sahara. And, don't forget that sand, whatever its other qualities, is at least sterile.

3 No one seems to know quite how many horses were around in the big cities in those days but if Daimler and Ford and the rest had not come along then today's figure would have to be ten, perhaps twenty 20
times as big. As incomes increased and general living standards rose the demand for 'personalised transport' would be bound to have kept pace.

4 The resulting hazard to health could only have been met by vastly increasing the number of crossing sweepers. At some busy junctions 25
one could visualise them standing shoulder to shoulder.

5 A strike of crossing sweepers would have been unthinkable – far more devastating than anything air traffic control assistants could wreak. Thus their industrial clout would have been enormous. No incomes policy could have stood against it. 30

6 So national economic ruin would seem one inevitable consequence and, of course, North Sea oil would have been no help since there would have been no use for it except to oil the carriage wheels. But what about less cosmic aspects of a society where horsepower means just that and no more? If you look at the normal car 35
commuter's daily routine we should get some idea.

7 As things stand it's out of the front door into the warm, dry, radio-filled cocoon of the car all the way to the office car park or, at worst,

the nearest vacant meter space. How different if you had first to catch your horse – which, of course would only be the beginning. Next 40 would come the saddling and bridling or the harnessing.

8   Next the inspection – or should it have been before? Is that a greasy hock? Is it firing on its pasterns? Is that a cough or croup? Aren't those the the signs of incipient thrush? Then the wet or windy ride to work with no chance of a quick, furtive shave at the traffic 45 lights and no chance to catch up with the news or weather reports before you arrived at the office stables.

9   Did Victorian offices and factories have stables or did some menial take your horse at the door and lead it to some livery establishment? I don't know but imagine an underground office stable below one of 50 our modern blocks!

10   Or perhaps you'd rather imagine a suburban Sunday morning scene where smart cobs and handy hackneys have replaced the Cortinas and Marinas. All that mucking out and swilling down and curry combing and drenching and douching and not a moment to 55 spare for the colour supplements and hardly time to get to the pub and then too tired to keep awake for Soccer Highlights on the telly.

11   And that's only the private sector. Think of the delay on a horse bus with the driver trying to give change while holding two pairs of reins. Put yourself in the place of an expectant mother in a horse- 60 drawn ambulance and try to imagine waiting for a horse-drawn fire engine.

12   Would there, then, be no compensations? No motorways for a start and no flyovers. Rather less noise, if far more smells. More organically grown food for those who care for such things. It would 65 be hard for the Government to tax grass which might keep down the cost of transport – though they could, and almost certainly would, tax corn. Insurance claims might be more fun to fill in and there would be less 'one-upmanship' from acquiring the latest model.

13   Ah, yes, and there could be one thing more – a new national poet 70 and playwright. Did not Shakespeare learn much of what he knew about life while holding horses' heads?

———————

1   **a**   Did you find this passage more or less persuasive than 'Staying Alive'? Why?

     b   Which one or more of these terms could be used to describe

        (i) the **tone** of the passage:
           solemn, lyrical, witty, angry, whimsical?

(ii) the presentation of the topic:
factual, imaginative, rational, subtle, exaggerated?

2 a An overseas reader might have some difficulty with

(i) **colloquialisms** like 'revving' *(line 4)*
(ii) **allusions** like 'Bank Holiday' *(line 1)* 'Piccadilly' *(line 15)*
(iii) **technical terms** like 'pastern' *(line 43)*.

Find two more of each category and write footnotes explaining them.

b (i) The terms 'juggernaut' *(line 4)* and 'centaur' ('Staying Alive' *line 110*) are from cultures removed from our own. Give or find their meaning and say why they are aptly used in these passages.
(ii) Find the origin of the following:
charisma, blitzkrieg, Mecca, filibuster, triumvirate, and suggest a present-day context for each.

3 Write a piece mocking the nostalgic appeal of one of these:

a steam trains
b kitchen cooking ranges
c horn gramophones
d early cameras
e oil lamps
f any similar topic of your own choice.

3 John, Me and the Lancashire Treasure

Ray Connolly

Ray Connolly was born in Lancashire in 1940. He took a degree in social anthropology at the London School of Economics in 1963 and has worked as a journalist since 1964, first for the *Liverpool Daily Post* and then *The Evening Standard* in London. He has also contributed to *The Sunday Times* (as guest Atticus), *The Observer*, *The Daily Mail*, *Vogue* and several other women's magazines. He is the author of seven novels, six television plays and two films: *That'll Be The Day* and *Stardust*. He has also written and directed a documentary film on James Dean. He is married with three children and lives in London.

---

1 I learned the real meaning of *gold fever* when I was thirteen – although in my case the fever was silver and came in the shape of thirty-three Roman coins dug out of the bed of a small stream on a West Lancashire farm.

2   A chance remark by a friend of my sister's that a hoard of coins   *5* had once been discovered about two miles from where I lived turned me, and my lifelong friend John Rimmer, into obsessive archaeologists and pubescent criminals. Our logic went: if 100 coins had been found there already then surely there must be a few more lying around undiscovered. There were, but getting at them was murder,   *10* and the idea of handing them over to some local museum as treasure trove was risible.

3   The trouble was that the Roman soldier, or whoever had originally owned them, had chosen the side of a stream in which to bury them. (Possibly he had won them gambling, since they were all   *15* denarii.) But unfortunately during the next nineteen hundred years or so the stream had slightly changed course until the coins were embedded in its bank or buried in the silt in the bottom.

4   When we first went coining it was the Easter holidays. Equipped with huge shovels and riddles which we borrowed from the local   *20* farm we began the spine-bending task of shovelling silt from the bottom of the stream into a riddle, carefully carrying the riddle to a place where the water flowed more quickly, washing out the mud and then staring like gypsies into tea leaves at the remaining collection of

9

tiny pebbles for the dull grey discs we had been told about. 25

5   By mid-afternoon we were beginning to wonder whether some cruel joke had been played upon us and we took to catching tiddlers in our vacuum flasks, chasing the cows back from our site and hurling chunks of mud after a trespassing water rat. At tea-time when our hearts were hardly in it the boy from the local farm paid us 30 a visit. It was he who had originally discovered the treasure.

6   'How many have you got?' he asked locanically, leaning over the handlebars of his bicycle. 'None,' we answered dejectedly, half afraid even to look at him.

7   He grunted, climbed from his bicycle and clambered down the 35 bank. 'You're digging in the wrong place,' he said, 'You should be more over here.' And taking my shovel from me he quickly filled the riddle full of silt, washed it out and began to sift through the remains. Suddenly his hand shot forward like the tongue of a snake. 'There you are,' he said, 'That's one!' 40

8   He passed me a dull grey piece of metal about the size of a sixpence. It was a coin, but not much of a coin. 'You have it,' he said, 'and dig in the right place next time.' And with that he climbed back on his bike and pedalled away up the field. Putting the coin carefully into a purse we had brought for our anticipated treasure, we 45 returned to our work with renewed enthusiasm. Before the day was out we had actually found a couple of our own, although none of them would have convinced a doubter. Nineteen hundred years had erased all their markings.

9   The next day we hit the jackpot. From virtually the first riddle we 50 pulled out three almost perfect coins, probably as clearly marked as when they had been originally buried. They were a Nerva, a Hadrian and a Trajan. We had actually found treasure, proper treasure, with heads and names impressed upon it.

10   But suddenly the easy camaraderie which we had shared for years 55 became stretched with tension as jealousy crept in.

11   We would peer together over the riddle, each desperate to spot the next coin before the other. And now we began to make our own separate collections as more Nervas came in, more Hadrians and even an Augustus Caesar. We had found the coins which had been 60 overlooked, but, like a couple of gold crazy prospectors, mutual distrust and envy had taken over. Had one of us had a gun he might easily have decided to dispatch the other and claim the booty as his own.

12   For two weeks we worked that stream. 65

13   By now, of course, the whole river bank looked like something out of the Klondike, as heaps of rubble were tipped upon the grass after examination. We were less than pleased when the farmer's son came

with the news that his father would like us to tidy up before we finished. By now we must have collected over twenty coins and we would pore over reference books in John's house trying to trace exactly what kind of coins we had found. *70*

14   We went coining again in the summer holidays, but now it was a case of diminishing returns. We had scooped most of the ones that had got away and only a handful more were added to our collection. *75* At Christmas we tried to work in a stream swollen by heavy snow and although we found three more on one lucky day, our fingers were so swollen and red we could hardly pluck them out of the riddle.

15   Then a strange thing happened: I lost one, and with it I lost interest. I know I had it on the bus going to school. But when I got *80* there it had gone. John was livid. He was convinced I'd given it to the bus conductor by mistake.

16   All the fun of finding the coins was souring our friendship, so one day I just put all my share into a handkerchief, wrapped it up and gave it to my friend. 'You'd better keep them,' I said. 'I don't trust *85* myself not to lose the lot.'

17   It was true, I didn't. And anyway, I had all kinds of new hobbies to be getting on with: there was chicken farming (all fifty died on me), mushroom growing, sword-collecting (my mother eventually gave them to a house decorator) and rock and roll. The fun had been *90* *finding* the coins. John was a much better bank than I was.

18   I went to see him a couple of years ago. He lives in New Zealand now and keeps them in a safe, all carefully labelled – apart from three very rare ones which apparently even foxed the British Museum. And apparently Paki-Has and Maoris come from miles *95* around to see this grand collection.

19   With great pride he carefully got them out for me and spread them across the dining table as we reminisced about who found which ones. At last, with some trepidation, I asked whether I might have one. *100*

20   'One!' he said in astonishment. 'You can take half of them. Choose any fifteen. They're yours. I've only been looking after them for you until you came to your senses.'

21   I chose one. It was one I remembered finding. I still didn't trust myself with the rest. Apparently they're worth over £1,000 now and *105* going up in value all the time.

22   It's a pretty wonderful thing to be thirteen years old and find buried treasure.

From *The Sunday Times*, 13 June, 1980

1 a The word 'treasure' has a variety of **connotations** or **overtones**. Give two or three **contexts** where you might meet the word and the different meanings it carries in each case.

b Show how paragraphs 10, 15 and 18 mark important stages in the account.

c What does the author gain by italicising the word 'finding' *(line 91)*?

2 a (i) Test your vocabulary by stating or guessing the meaning of:

'risible' *(line 12)* 'laconically' *(line 32)* 'dejectedly' *(line 33)* 'virtually' *(line 50)* 'impressed' *(line 54)* 'camaraderie' *(line 55)* 'returns' *(line 74)* 'foxed' *(line 94)* 'reminisced' *(line 98)* 'trepidation' *(line 99.)*.

(ii) Select the two least familiar words in the list and suggest ways of fixing their meaning in one's mind.

b The humour of the passage often depends on **implication** or **allusion**. Suggest how this is the case for:

   (i) 'obsessive archaeologists and pubescent criminals' *(lines 7–8)*
  (ii) 'they were all denarii' *(lines 15–16)*
 (iii) 'coining' *(line 19)*
 (iv) 'spine-bending' *(line 21)*
  (v) 'staring like gypsies into tea-leaves' *(line 24)*
 (vi) 'a trespassing water rat' *(line 29)*
 (vii) 'hit the jackpot' *(line 50)*
(viii) 'something out of the Klondike' *(lines 66–67)*
 (ix) 'scooped' *(line 74)*
  (x) 'John was a much better bank than I was' *(line 91)*.

3 'These amateur treasure hunters with their metal detectors are selfishly destroying sites of great archaeological interest.'

'The amateur treasure hunters have discovered hundreds of objects that the professionals would never have time or money to find.'

Which side in this argument would you support? Add two further points to back up your case.

4 Breeding Out Faults

Gerald Leach

Gerald Leach was born in 1933 and has been a science writer for most of his career. During the 1960s he presented, wrote and produced television science programmes for ITV and the BBC, edited the science magazine *Discovery*, was science correspondent for the *New Statesman*, and wrote several popular science books apart from *The Biocrats*. From 1969 to 1972 he was science correspondent for *The Observer*, where he became increasingly interested in problems of the environment, population, resources and developing countries. Since 1972 he has been at the International Institute for Environment and Development, in London, working on energy conservation and energy policies. Apart from many papers and articles, during this time he has written two widely quoted books on *Energy and Food Production* and *A Low Energy Strategy for the United Kingdom*. He is married with two children and lives in Hampstead and Gloucestershire.

1 Most of us produce babies with as much idea of what kind we are going to get as a child dipping for a present in a bran tub – and with the same mixture of hope and fear of disappointment. We set a couple of hundred million sperm after an egg whose genes we know just as little about and then wait nine months, or years, to know if we 5 have won or lost the inheritance lottery.

2 Most of us win. Though we all carry lethal or crippling genes in our gonads, we have normal children. Luck is on our side. But sometimes the genetic fruit-machine presents a combination that spells catastrophe. At least one in every eight established embryos is 10 killed by its genetic defects. One in every forty or so babies is stillborn or dies within a year because of birth hazards or congenital defects. Worst of all, about one in twenty-five babies is born with a physical or mental handicap and *lives*. In Britain alone these living survivors of cruel accidents of inheritance, development and birth arrive at the 15 rate of around five hundred a week and add up to a total handicapped population of about two million. Though by no means all are gravely disabled, together they comprise one of the principal causes of human suffering.

3 In the next few years biology and medicine are going to give us the 20 chance of reducing this misery. Not eliminating it, but cutting it dramatically. As they lay bare the genetic and chemical machinery of man, they will accumulate techniques that could be used to cure or

13

prevent a great many kinds of birth defect. But whether we seize the chance they offer is a different matter, because before we can we shall *25* have to change quite drastically our attitudes to many traditional practices and 'rights'. Few of these techniques will come without changes, sacrifices and expense. It is not therefore just a matter of novel means; once again biomedicine is challenging us to think very carefully indeed about ends, and to decide what it is we really want to *30* do.

4   One of the biggest challenges (and the main theme of this chapter) is that in the near future we shall – or could if we wanted to – know a great deal more about the 'bad' genes we all carry. This is the challenge of negative eugenics. When we have this genetic fore- *35* knowledge and *know* the risk we run of producing a defective child, what are we going to do? Ultimately, if we ever achieve the necessary technical wizardry, we may be able to take our genes along to the genetic surgeon and have them 'cured'. But in the meantime the responsibility of this new knowledge will hang heavy, because as *40* long as we have to reproduce with the genes we have, unaltered, genetic foreknowledge will force us to ask ourselves whom we dare marry and have children by, or whether we dare have children at all. And bearing in mind the fantastic cost of coping with birth defects, it may force society to answer the questions for us by 'advising' us what *45* to do.

From *The Biocrats*

---

1 **a** The author makes the **assertion** that physically and mentally handicapped people 'comprise one of the principal causes of human suffering' *(lines 18–19)*.

      Give *one* argument in support of and *one* argument against this view.

  b The chance of reducing the misery of handicapped people depends, the writer suggests, on two factors *(lines 22–24)* which in turn depend on various conditions *(lines 25–31)*.

      State the two factors and three of the conditions.

  c (i) Deduce from its **context** the meaning of the phrase 'negative eugenics' *(line 35)*.

    (ii) How is the word 'eugenics' related to the words 'gene' and 'genetic'?

d   (i) What are the 'means' *(line 29)* and the 'ends' *(line 30)* the writer refers to?

    (ii) Invent a case where in your view the end does *not* justify the means.

2   **a**   An **analogy** compares items that are similar in some respects.

    (i) Explain the similarities involved in the analogy in lines 1–3.

    (ii) What dissimilarities does the analogy *not* take account of?

    (iii) What **metaphors** in paragraphs 1 and 2 continue the analogy?

  b   Explain the metaphors carried by the words 'machinery' *(line 22)* and 'wizardry' *(line 38)*.

    Say which you consider the more effective, and why.

  c   Choose two of these words and explain why the writer puts them in inverted commas: 'rights' *(line 27)* 'bad' *(line 34)* 'cured' *(line 39)* 'advising' *(line 45)*.

3   **a**   The last two sentences *(lines 39–46)* carry certain **implications** for the future. Say what these are and give the comment on them which (i) an optimist (ii) a pessimist might make.

  b   Aldous Huxley's novel *Brave New World* pictures a future society where embryos are reared in bottles and conditioned to perform their role in society without question, and sex is promiscuous and purely for pleasure.

    Say with reasons whether you think this state of affairs (i) will (ii) should come about.

5 The Looking Glass Kids
David Lewis

David Lewis was born in London in 1942 and educated in France, Britain and the USA. He has a first class honours degree in psychology, a BA in communications studies and an MSc in brain studies. He is a consultant and research psychologist, clinical director of Stresswatch, a non-profit making organisation which helps people with anxiety and phobic problems, and the author of several books on child psychology. He originally studied medicine before changing to a psychology degree and obtaining special qualifications in psychometrics. His early writing for the popular, as opposed to the academic, press included an investigation of the conviction for murder of two London men, Dennis Stafford and Michael Luvaglio. The book made legal history when the campaign it initiated led to the case being referred back to the Court of Appeal. His psychological books include *The Secret Language of Your Child*, a study of infant body language, and *Teach Your Child Greater Intelligence*, published by Souvenir Press in 1981. He broadcasts and lectures widely both in Europe and the United States.

1 Michael's father believes children should be able to stand up for themselves and fight back. Michael's father enjoys boxing and so will five-year-old Michael. Clara's mother is an enthusiast for classical music and despises 'pop'. The only music Clara is ever allowed to listen to, or has been allowed to listen to during her four years of life, 5
are the classics. Billy's father is convinced of the superiority of the white race and the inferiority of all others. At the age of five Billy already shares his father's prejudices. Mary's mother thinks that the children in their neighbourhood are too common for her daughter to play with. Four-year-old Mary thinks they are common as well. 10
2 These are the 'looking glass kids'. They are being brought up to reflect only their parents' view of the world. If, as they grow older and experience other attitudes and opinions, they shatter the mirror and start to think for themselves the parents will probably be upset and angry. 15
'How could Mike refuse to go on boxing? Is he a sissy?'
'How could Clara want to listen to that rubbish? Has she no taste?'
'How could Billy date a girl from another culture? Has he no pride?'
3 If the parental pressures are strong enough, these rejections of the hand-me-down attitudes may never occur, or be short-lived if they 20

do. In any event, it is most unlikely that the children will have sufficient knowledge of the world to reject them, or even seriously question them, before the age of five. During these vital years of development their perceptions of the world will accurately mirror those of their parents. Since the parents are the child's major source *25* of knowledge and information about the world, such a sharing of viewpoints is inevitable. But that does not mean it must consist only of those values which the adults perceive as important. For the child to progress successfully it must enjoy, as early as possible and as often as possible, the widest possible access to different viewpoints. *30* Children should certainly be exposed to the special interests and deeply-felt beliefs of their parents, but not to the exclusion of all else and never in such a way that alternatives are held up as being unworthy of their attention or interest.

4   It is always very hard to become aware of one's own prejudices, or *35* to consider deeply-felt attitudes as being just one of a number of possible viewpoints. Usually they seem so 'right' and 'natural' that it becomes impossible even to consider that viable alternatives may exist. Part of the skill of the gifted parent lies in an ability to expose the child to as wide as possible a variety of ideas, opinions, attitudes *40* and possibilities. In this way they come to reflect experience brilliantly and in all directions, like a many-faceted diamond rather than the single image of the looking glass.

5   Some parents may feel that it is wrong to allow a child below the age of five to make up his, or her, mind about anything of *45* importance. They might argue that nobody so lacking in knowledge and experience of the world has any right to make a decision on anything significant. Far better for the parents to do the thinking for the child and to hand over a neatly-packaged answer. An additional criticism which some parents have voiced to me is that children *50* become very anxious when there is any degree of uncertainty. By offering a variety of experiences and possibilities you merely confuse and bewilder the child. It is far safer to provide ready-made verities on which they can build their perceptions of life. Certainly, some children need more reassurance than others. They tend to become *55* anxious when faced with the unusual and take longer to adapt to new situations. But this does not mean they cannot be provided with a range of experiences, so long as it is done sensitively and in constant sympathy with the child's particular needs. How the task is to be accomplished must be a matter for individual parents. Only they *60* have the expert knowledge of their own children necessary for judging the best approach. But playing safe is certainly not the answer if the child's mind is to be allowed to develop.

6   It should be made clear that I am not saying children must be

discouraged from sharing their parents' interests, nor should adults *65*
be concerned about expressing their own honest views about life.
Maybe the children will find them equally convincing and adopt
those interests and attitudes as their own. But the choice has to be
theirs, and it can only properly be made once the child has been
allowed to experience as many viewpoints as possible. *70*

7   If the child is persistently moulded to reflect the opinions and
attitudes of the adult then a close replica will almost certainly result.
But that independence of thought and self-confident awareness so
necessary for successful mental growth will be restricted. Under
these conditions it is much less likely that the child's inborn potential *75*
can ever be achieved.

From *How to be a Gifted Parent*

1 **a** (i) The **metaphor** in the title and line 13 is developed in four
          other places in the passage. Find these points and say how
          each illustrates the main argument.
       (ii) In paragraph 3 there is a metaphor of similar meaning. Say
          what it is and whether you think it effective.

   b If Mary's parents were 'upset and angry' *(lines 14–15)* what
       question might they ask about her?

   c What is the author's answer, in paragraphs 3 and 4, to the point
       raised in paragraphs 1 and 2, and what **qualification** does he add
       in lines 58–59?

   d Briefly give the two arguments *(lines 46–53)* which the author
       admits parents might make against him.

2 **a** The passage begins with a number of **examples** or **illustrations**.
       Invent three others which would support the author's argument.

   b (i) How does the use of the word 'but' in lines 27, 57, 62, 68 and
          73 help the author's argument?
       (ii) What point does the writer **concede** by the use of the word
          'certainly' *(line 62)?*
       (iii) Find three other words or phrases that seem to you
          important in emphasising the run of the argument.

18

3 a Give an example, in yourself or a person you know, of one 'prejudice' and one 'deeply felt attitude' *(line 36)*.

b Write a dialogue in which a grown-up son or daughter criticises a parent for giving him/her too little or too much freedom to form individual opinions.

6 Rebel Daughter
Mary Kenny

Mary Kenny was born in Dublin and has been a reporter, feature writer, columnist, foreign correspondent and executive on newspapers. At present she writes regularly for *The New Standard, Cosmopolitan* and *The Daily Express*. The problems of pursuing a career while being a mother and running a home are explored in her book *Woman x Two* (1978).

1 Which woman has not been a rebel daughter at one stage or another?
2   In my case, it all began when I was sent to boarding school. Irish children generally are not sent away to school as much as English children, because the idea of the family unit is still very strong in Ireland, and the family is still thought of as the best environment for *5* a child. However, by the time I was fourteen I was becoming what is called 'out of hand'. Though a charming little girl, I had always been naughty and odious: 'bold as brass' they called me, and everyone agreed that I needed a good dose of boarding school.
3   So off I went, togged out in my new uniform and armed with *10* chock-a-block tuck box and impressive-looking hockey stick. And unknowingly, I said good-bye to my mother in a very final way.
4   My universe became school; I made new friends, encountered new experiences and lived a life divorced from associations with mother. About this time, I developed a strong crush on a sixth-former who *15* played a spectacular game of hockey and could do all the things that I most wanted to be able to do, i.e., be very cheeky to the nuns and swear in French. Psychiatrists might say I was searching for a mother-replacement figure or *ersatz* and typically of my generation, I respect what psychiatrists have to say. Looking back now I believe *20* that if I had had some psycho-analysis at fifteen, I might have been saved a lot of problems. Freud has percolated so far into our common thinking today, that we talk – often unknowingly – in terms of Freud all the time.
5   When I returned home for the long summer vacation, I was more *25* insupportable than ever. I really was the nastiest teenager you could ever meet: aggressive, violent, awkward, tactless – a constant source of embarrassment to people. With mother, I was beyond reason. I continually criticised her, corrected her and quarrelled with her every day. I even threw her own china at her. Everybody said I was a *30*

terror, and of course they were right. But they were judging on behaviour, with little insight into my interior problems.

6   My main interior problem was, I think, that mother had ceased to be the infallible goddess she had seemed, and I felt specially insecure. When I was a small child, mother seemed very beautiful to me, smelt *35* delicious, and made everything all right by her very presence. My father died when I was five but mother was always there. When you were sick, she seemed to cure you magically, and when you said, 'Mummy, will I die tonight?' (Catholic prayers have a lot about 'And if I die before I wake . . .') she would answer, 'Of course you won't *40* die tonight', and her word was truth in the absolute degree. Irrevocable.

7   And then suddenly it all changes. Mother may still be an attractive woman, but you know she is growing old. She can't cure you of the things that matter most to you – now you have to cure them *45* yourself – and even her word, your reason tells you now, is no guarantee against death. So much about her seems to be wrong, and you resent that. Sometimes you're ashamed of her if she comes to the door with her apron on, or if you see her without her dentures, and you disapprove of a whole lot of things about her. Maybe the way *50* she speaks, or the way she dresses, or something you had never even noticed before. When you introduce her to your friends, you are in an inner agony lest she do the wrong thing. And like the girls in Mary McCarthy's book, *The Group*, you want to be different from her.

8   It's all very primitive and natural I suppose. It is the old order of *55* the young bird trying its wings and flying out of the nest. If we did not reject our mothers, we would never have the courage to leave them.

9   This conflict with my mother continued on and off all through my adolescence, although by the time I was seventeen it had begun to abate. When I was eighteen I left Ireland. I remember weeping in *60* Mother's arms as my uncle was waiting to take me to the boat. 'For heaven's sake, you silly child,' she consoled me in a practical voice. 'Do you want to stay by your mother's side all your life and be a failure?' In her immense wisdom, she knew I had to try it all out for myself, but there were tears in her eyes too. *65*

10   Now, of course, at the august age of twenty-one, and a professional young woman in London, all that's over and I have a better-than-ever relationship with my mother. I can really appreciate her as a person, and though I can recognise her shortcomings too, yet I believe that I am going back to my original childhood vision of *70* her perfection. Of course we still have arguments; only the other day I was trying to convince her that chastity was an outdated virtue which the modern world had happily dispensed with. Can you imagine mother swallowing that?

11   And yet I can still be her little girl again, and ring her up in tears,   *75*
crying, 'Oh, mammy, I'm so miserable and my heart is broken,' and
she will say with all that old assurance which brought you the
absolute truth in your childhood anxiety – 'Dear child, I broke my
heart a thousand times before I met your father. Now dry your eyes
and don't fret.'   *80*
12   It must be bewildering and saddening for a mother to have a rebel
daughter and to see her own child grow away from her, but
afterwards, when the rebel is not so much quelled, as brought round
to reason by sheer experience, it can result in a much more profitable
relationship.   *85*

From *Woman's Hour: a Selection*

1 **a** This essay could be subdivided into two, three or four sections.

(i) How would you divide it?
(ii) Summarise in a sentence each subdivision you have made.

b Show the relevance of the following to the main theme of the
essay:

(i) 'I needed a good dose of boarding school' *(line 9)*
(ii) the 'sixth-former who played a spectacular game of hockey'
(line 15–16)
(iii) 'I even threw her own china at her' *(line 30)*
(iv) 'she seemed to cure you magically' *(line 38)*
(v) 'chastity was an outdated virtue' *(line 72)*.

c What would be lost if the first and last paragraphs were omitted?

2 **a** A **rhetorical question** is one used for emphasis and not usually
requiring an answer. Which of the questions in paragraphs 1, 6, 9
and 10 belong to this type?

b Why does the writer change from

(i) 'When I' *(line 35)* to 'When you' *(line 37)*
(ii) the past to the present tense *(paragraphs 6 and 7)*?

c (i) Place the following into the **categories** of **formal** or **informal**:

'the best environment' *(line 5)* 'bold as brass' *(line 8)* 'a good dose' *(line 9)* 'divorced from associations' *(line 14)*.

(ii) Find two other examples of each category.

(iii) Decide whether the passage (excluding the conversation) becomes more or less formal as it proceeds.

(iv) Say why you think this is so.

d Say whether the following **inferences** can or cannot be reasonably drawn from the passage:

(i) Freudian psychology has been a harmful influence.

(ii) We should not judge people entirely on what they do.

(iii) All girls become disillusioned about their mothers.

(iv) Every generation is different from the previous one.

(v) Sons grow away from their fathers.

(vi) Attitudes are modified by experience.

e Why is the phrase 'at the august age of twenty one' *(line 66)* **ironic**?

3 a Must we reject our mothers?

b Write a fragment from a novel concerning Mary Kenny's home life or school life. Decide whether a first-person or third-person narrative would be more effective.

7 The Tribe That Has Lost its Way
Jill Tweedie

Jill Tweedie is widely known as a journalist. Her work often deals with controversial issues, for example the relationship between the sexes or the generations in contemporary society. She has had a weekly column in *The Guardian* for ten years and has received both Granada Television and IPC awards for being 'Best Journalist of the Year'. She has also made many broadcasts on radio and television and was presenter of Thames TV 'Good Afternoon' for two years. In 1980 she published *In the Name of Love*, a study of the concepts of love and marriage.

1 Here are the lads, fourteen and sixteen, grimacing and gibbering at the table, huge feet splayed across the floor, huge elbows a threat to every glass and dish. One displays upon his silly head two white swathes of scalp intersected by a cockscomb of Woolworth-dyed hair, the other has no hair at all. Their rubber faces, volcanic with   5
spots, pack in features from a spilled Identikit – here the high curved forehead and dimpled chin of a toddler, there a man's nose and bristly upper lip. The voices, half rough, half squeaky, boom monotonously on. 'Shut your gob,' says one and both collapse at their own wit, beating the table, flapping their arms, croaking like   10
dying camels.
2   Exhausted, we plead with them to go and they comply, lolloping across the room, thin and long as celery in their tattered vests and holey jeans, chimps leaving the tea party. My companion, their sister, a fifteen-year-old with shining, well-brushed tresses, im-   15
maculate jeans and a University of Leeds top, regards their capering backs with loathing. Patting her, I say, 'Take no notice, love. They're only boys,' and she turns on me in aggrieved bewilderment. 'Why do you *say* that?' she says. 'What do you *mean*, they're only boys?'
3   I have the fleeting impression that if I could answer that question   20
I would have solved the riddle of the Sphinx. The girl beside me – sociable, intelligent, restrained, reliable – is already uneasily aware that somehow she seems to be losing out to these two hominoids who hold, in their chewed and meaty hands, the beginnings of the *entrée* they will have as males to all the world's   25
business, from God to Mammon. Only boys grow up into only men, and only men rule the world.

4   They mirror chaos, these adolescent boys, their gawky bodies and
lunatic behaviour a reflection of all we no longer need in that world.
And this despite the much-vaunted power of Motherhood that has, *30*
since they were born, impressed upon them the manners and values
of a gentler civilisation, partly for self-preservation and partly out of
the deepest conviction of future necessity. Mother thought she had
won, poor foolish Mother. They were going on nicely for the first
twelve years: affectionate, kind, a joy to see in their charming Colts *35*
clothes and Persil-white Arans.

5   And then came the thirteenth birthday. Overnight, the trolls stole
away our pretty sons and left us changelings instead, Neander-
thalers, throwbacks to some noisome cave, the land around made
hideous with their battle cries and scufflings for territory.   *40*

6   Old men, said the poet, know when an old man dies but every one
of us knows when young men begin to live. They erupt all around us,
howling in football stadiums, slashing train seats, mugging old ladies
or, at best, hanging about street corners frightening the horses and if
you think I'm exaggerating, read the statistics. It is, anyway, an *45*
unwritten law of life that no two boys between twelve and sixteen can
be together more than three minutes without lying to each other,
putting each other down, punching each other *or all three at once*,
hard. Who, I ask myself, watching them, needs them? What are they
for?   *50*

7   The so-called primitive peoples knew and still know. Adolescent
males are for putting in the Long Hut among their own kind, well
away from the rest of the tribe. They are for sticking feathers in their
hair and painting their faces with the colours of battle. They are for
jigging up and down until they fall exhausted, pushing spikes *55*
through their cheeks or walking over red-hot cinders without crying.
In other words, they are for learning the skills and obligations of
hunting and killing, whether for food or defence or territory,
whether against animals or other males. But that was long ago and
far away. We don't need hunters or warriors in Finsbury Park or *60*
downtown Manhattan or, for that matter, downtown Kampala. We
need them as little as the hole in the head they will quite likely give us
but, so far, that evolutionary message doesn't seem to have got
through too well. Indeed today's adolescent boys, deprived of
socially sanctioned rituals, are busy inventing and re-inventing their *65*
own as instinctively and compulsively as soldier ants in a hill. At the
vast, impersonal insistence of their atavistic genes and kind, they
force themselves and other boys to confront a fearful enemy and the
fearful enemy turns out to be themselves.

From *The Observer*, 28 October, 1979

1 a Give the comments you might hear on this extract from two males and two females of different ages.

b Consider the questions near the end of paragraphs 2 and 6, rephrase them as one general question and give *your* answer.

c What might we find in 'the statistics' *(line 45)*?

d What **implication** is carried in the phrase 'or, for that matter, downtown Kampala' *(line 61)*?

e How do you interpret ' . . . the fearful enemy turns out to be themselves' *(lines 68–69)*?

2 a Say whether you find the general **tone** of the extract serious or humorous. Give reasons.

b (i) Explain the **allusions** in:

'grimacing and gibbering' *(line 1)* 'chimps leaving the tea party' *(line 14)* 'hominoids' *(line 24)*.

(ii) Say what these items have in common and why the writer introduces them.

(iii) Find two more items in paragraph 5 and one in paragraph 6 which develop the same idea.

c Which **epithets** (not already covered in **b**) describing the boys seem to you most or least apt?

d (i) Which ideas are placed in **opposition** by the use of the word 'but' *(line 59)*?

(ii) It might be argued there is also a **contradiction** in this paragraph (7). Show that there is or is not.

3 a Write two entries about boys from the diary of the fifteen-year old girl *(paragraph 2)*

(i) as she is now
(ii) at some future date.

b Which one or more of the following words would you apply to lines 23–27 (' . . . she seems to be losing out . . . only men rule the world.'):

(i) true (ii) false (iii) ironic (iv) sexist?

c In the latter part of her article, which describes the 'boot boys', 'soul boys', 'punks', 'rockabillies' and other adolescent boys in the London scene, Jill Tweedie makes these comments. Discuss *one* of them:

  (i) 'Do they live in fear of one another or do they, to some extent at least, enjoy that fear?'
  (ii) 'As an adult I shudder at them but, more often, I shudder for them. They are fragile little coracles bobbing up and down, each one rowing like mad in the face of a tidal wave, and there is no help at hand upon the unfriendly banks.'
  (iii) 'We, the dying generations, turn our backs upon them, cursing their excesses while refusing even to imagine ways in which their once-vital genetic heritage could be leavened for our common wealth.'

8 Childhood Discipline

Margaret Mead

Born in Philadelphia, Pennsylvania, in 1901, Margaret Mead won research fellowships which enabled her to study primitive cultures in Oceania. As a result she published two books – *Coming of Age in Samoa* (1928) and *Growing Up in New Guinea* (1931) – which gained her an international reputation in anthropology. Other notable works among her prolific output are *Male and Female* (1949), a study of American sexual attitudes in the light of her Pacific researches, *New Lives for Old* (1956), a further study of the Manus people of New Guinea, and *An Anthropologist at Work* (1959). *Some Personal Views* is a collection of her opinions on almost every conceivable topic, given over a number of years. She died in 1978.

1 Of all the societies of which you have firsthand knowledge, which has the most effective means of disciplining its children and which has the least? What are those methods?

AUGUST 1967

2   In the matter of childhood disciplines there is no absolute standard. *5* The question is one of appropriateness to a style of living. What is the intended outcome? Are the methods of discipline effective in preparing the child to live in the adult world into which he is growing? The means of discipline that are very effective in rearing children to become headhunters and cannibals would be most *10* ineffective in preparing them to become peaceful shepherds.

3   The Mundugumor, a New Guinea people, trained their children to be tough and self-reliant. Among these headhunters, when one village was preparing to attack another and wanted to guard itself against attack by a third village, the first village sent its children to *15* the third to be held as hostages. The children knew that they faced death if their own people broke this temporary truce. Mundugumor methods of child rearing were harsh but efficient. An infant sleeping in a basket hung on the wall was not taken out and held when it wakened and cried. Instead, someone scratched on the outside of the *20* basket, making a screeching sound like the squeak of chalk on a blackboard. And a child that cried with fright was not given the mother's breast. It was simply lifted and held off the ground. Mundugumor children learned to live in a tough world, unfearful of

hostility. When they lived among strangers as hostages, they 25
watched and listened, gathering the information they would need
someday for a successful raid on this village.

4   The Arapesh, another New Guinea people had a very different
view of life and human personality. They expected their children to
grow up in a fairly peaceful world, and their methods of caring for 30
children reflected their belief that both men and women were gentle
and nurturing in their intimate personal relations. Parents re-
sponded to an infant's least cry, held him and comforted him. And
far from using punishment as a discipline, adults sometimes stood
helplessly by while a child pitched precious firewood over a cliff.   35

5   Even very inconsistent discipline may fit a child to live in an
inconsistent world. A Balinese mother would play on her child's
fright by shouting warnings against nonexistent dangers: 'Look out!
Fire! . . . Snake! . . . Tiger!' The Balinese system required people to
avoid strange places without inquiring why. And the Balinese child 40
learned simply to be afraid of strangeness. He never learned that
there are no bears under the stairs, as American children do. We
want our children to test reality. We teach our children to believe in
Santa Claus and later, without bitter disappointment, to give up that
belief. We want them to be open to change, and as they grow older, 45
to put childhood fears and rewards aside and be ready for new kinds
of reality.

6   There are also forms of discipline that may be self-defeating.
Training for bravery, for example, may be so rigorous that some
children give up in despair. Some Plains Indians put boys through 50
such severe and frightening experiences in preparing them for their
young manhood as warriors that some boys gave up entirely and
dressed instead as women.

7   In a society in which many people are socially mobile and may live
as adults in a social or cultural environment very different from the 55
one in which they grew up, old forms of discipline may be wholly
unsuited to new situations. A father whose family lived according to ·
a rigid, severe set of standards, and who was beaten in his boyhood
for lying or stealing, may still think of beating as an appropriate
method of disciplining his son. Though he now lives as a middle-class 60
professional man in a suburb, he may punish his son roughly for not
doing well in school. It is not the harshness as such that then may
discourage the boy even more, but his bewilderment. Living in a
milieu in which parents and teachers reward children by praise and
presents for doing well in school – a milieu in which beating is not 65
connected with competence in schoolwork – the boy may not be able
to make much sense of the treatment he receives.

8   There is still another consideration in this question about

29

discipline. Through studies of children as they grow up in different cultures we are coming to understand more about the supportive and 70 the maiming effects of various forms of discipline. Extreme harshness or insensitivity to the child may prepare it to survive in a harsh environment. But it also may cripple the child's ability to meet changing situations. And today we cannot know the kind of world the children we are rearing will live in as adults. For us, therefore, the 75 most important question to ask about any method of discipline is: |How will it affect the child's capacity to face change?|Will it give the child the kind of strength necessary to live under new and unpredictable conditions?|

9   An unyielding conscience may be a good guide to successful living 80 in a narrow and predictable environment. But it may become a heavy burden and a cruel scourge in a world in which strength depends on flexibility. Similarly, the kind of discipline that makes a child tractable, easy to bring up and easy to teach in a highly structured milieu, may fail to give the child the independence, courage and 85 curiosity he will need to meet the challenges in a continually changing situation. At the same time, the absence of forms of discipline that give a child a sense of living in an ordered world in which it is rewarding to learn the rules, whatever they may be, also may be maiming. A belief in one's own accuracy and a dependable 90 sense of how to find the patterning in one's environment are necessary parts of mature adaptation to new styles of living.

10   There is, in fact, no single answer to the problem of childhood discipline. But there is always the central question: For what future?

From *Some Personal Views*

1 a   (i) What general criterion does Margaret Mead suggest for judging methods of childhood discipline?
       (ii) Find the three questions where this criterion is made **explicit**.
       (iii) Find the two questions which apply the general criterion to situations of change.
       (iv) The usefulness of corporal punishment in schools might be judged by these criteria:

       Does it
       A   deter the culprit from repeating his offence?

B   help the culprit develop self-discipline?
C   deter others from committing the offence?
D   prevent disruptive pupils from interrupting the work of
    the class?
E   give the culprit a proper sense of guilt?
F   reinforce the concept of authority?
G   give a salutory shock without generating malice?

Say which of these criteria seem the most relevant in a
case of
(a) bullying
(b) impertinence
(c) another offence from your own experience.

(v) Which of the criteria above −A to G − might the defender of
     capital punishment invoke to justify its use?

b Would you prefer to be a child in the Mundugumor *(paragraph
3)*, Arapesh *(paragraph 4)*, Balinese *(paragraph 5)* or Plains
Indians *(paragraph 6)* societies? Say why, bearing in mind the
author's points in paragraph 2.

2 a (i) What **generalisation** is supported by the **example** of the
           father in lines 57–67?
       (ii) Give an example to support the generalisation about the
            effect of harshness *(lines 71–73)*.

b A key idea in paragraphs 7–9 is 'change'.

(i) Find six phrases which refer to this idea and
(ii) show how each paragraph develops the point.

3 Describe an imaginary family:
either the Blacks, whose household is 'a highly structured milieu'
which fails to give the children 'the independence, courage and
curiosity' they will need 'to meet the challenges in a continually
changing situation' *(lines 84–87)*.

or the Whites, where the children live in 'an ordered world in
which it is rewarding to learn the rules, whatever they may be'
(lines 88–89).

9 Pop

Tony Jasper

Tony Jasper is author of twenty-two books which cover either separately religion, contemporary music and education, or attempt a fusion of these subjects. He writes and broadcasts on these three fields for BBC and commercial radio stations with over 1000 programmes to his credit since the early Seventies. He writes weekly for *Music Week* and *The Manchester Evening News* and has rock music programmes broadcast by Radio Hallam and British Forces Broadcasting Service. He attended three Universities, London, Oxford and an American University (Washington DC) and has several degrees in theology and various American credits in studies of the Media. He is a Methodist lay preacher and speaks and preaches throughout the world in churches, Universities and colleges.

1 Crazy, just crazy. Call it what you like. School lunchtime. Three hundred or more thronging the gym. Total involvement. People taking off, laughing, crying, finding hands to hold, new dance steps to learn. Noise, noise, noise, but people talking clothes, shoes, pop stars. Some come running towards the turntable clutching grubby 5 bundles holding precious records. 'Play it, Sir, please!' 'Don't let anyone handle it!' 'Aren't the Four Tops just great?' 'Have you got the new one from the Beach Boys?' 'Susan wants to dance with you.' 'Look at that lot, aren't they good!' 'Got any reggae?' Most of them would not be able to write down what was happening or say how 10 they felt. Ask them and they shrug their shoulders. This is the way it is. There. Where it's happening. If you want to find out, come and join in. Throw your collar-studs away, eat your cuff-links! Relax, take it easy, give yourself, feel the sounds coming through! Do you always have to be asking questions? 15

2   'I feel pop music is detrimental to a true musical expression!'
'Aren't you playing down to them with all this stuff?'
'This is the kind of thing you get in Comprehensives!'
'What's the point of teaching when someone allows this to go on?'
'I must say, doing a school duty is fun when they're all safely in the 20 gym.'
'Did you see them? Like savages, animals.'

3   Hear Fr Louis Savary:

'There is really nothing outside the grasp of this kingdom. It responds to everything and everyone. It speaks at the same time to 25 the skinny near-genius and to the boy with only muscles to sell, to the long-haired shy girl and the cool swinger, to the social élite at the head table in the school cafeteria and the social rejects who eat alone in the corner by the sunless windows. It talks to the truant spending a May morning with a 'Marvel' comic under a tree in Central Park and 30 to the high-school drop-out who earns the right to life driving a big red tractor through oceans of wheat in Kansas.[1]'

4   Of course, everyone has his own idea of pop. Comments from films, newspapers, magazines, radio and television, give rise to stereotypes, often with little basis in reality. The cinema world shouts: 'She's a 35 sex-hungry Superfan . . . GROUPIE GIRL.' 'My God,' people cry, 'Pop is about sex, bad sex.' London's *Evening Standard*, 5 October 1970, page 3, has news of Janis Joplin, the girl who said, 'I'd rather have ten years of superhypermost than live to be seventy sitting in some goddam chair.' Dead, needle marks in her arm. Yes, drugs, and 40 a minute number who offer their bodies and distort their systems with chemical substances become the image. Pop is bad, evil, sinful.

5   Indeed, there is another side which doesn't sound so attractive, colourful. Wardour Street, London, in the early hours of a Sunday morning. The rock clubs are telling people to go home and get cool. 45 A police raid, a search for drugs and anyone under sixteen. A girl with her friend gets taken away. She writes:

'The fuss put as all in a cell. In the Westend fuss shop I got picked up with two girls. One of them had some pot on her she got rid of it on the bus, there were three girls in the same cell we were all picked up at 50 the . . . at 2.30.
    One of the girls were triping. We sat and told jookes the old woman outside told us to be quiet . . . more and more girls went, then she asked for me, my mother was downstairs and waiting for me. I wished I was dead.'   55

6   Monday she's at school. No war-paint, flares, choker and beads. Minds and heads remember the night before; shattering volume from speakers, galloping strobe lights, smell of joss sticks, grass, words from hard drug pushers, huddled groups on the floor, films flashing on the walls, smell of cooking, stale fat, verbal musical 60

[1] Louis Savary, *The Kingdom of the Downtown*, Paulist/Association Press: New York, 1966; p. 19.

shouting of the groups, their own participation in a series of furious unplanned movements as the body becomes ordered by the sound and for a time everything becomes lifted into something having no relationship to ordinary existence. And how can all this be related to a blackboard, an authoritarian teacher, a shop till, the letter to be *65* typed without being read?

7   'Pray God, not my daughter.' OK Mrs Brown, but don't get hung up on it. Campaign against the drugs, clean up some clubs, but if you want to wage battle against the music, you're wasting your time. It's one of the biggest things around, and not just for a London club. The *70* music is everywhere, both sides of the manmade iron curtain, not limited to people of your daughter's age but part of those in their twenties, even thirties, who first moved and screamed at Elvis Presley and Bill Haley, perhaps cried with Johnny Ray.

1   a   (i) Why does the author introduce the remarks given in paragraph 2?
   (ii) Who might the speaker be in each case?
   (iii) Reply to or comment on two of the remarks.

   b   Give the gist of the quotation from Louis Savary and say what the author might hope to gain by including it.

   c   'Pop is bad, evil, sinful' *(line 42)*. Whose point of view is this?

   d   'The author **concedes** that . . . but would claim that . . . ' Use this formula to give a one-sentence **summary** of the passage.

2   a   Try to analyse the **style** of the passage by considering:

   (i) the **register**, i.e. the author's choice of words and expressions
   (ii) the sentence structure
   (iii) whether the author addresses the reader in a detached or **emotive** manner.

   b   The passage could be called **rhetorical**, i.e. it seeks to persuade. In what respects do you find it successful or unsuccessful?

3   Script a TV interview with one of the people mentioned in the passage.

10 Child's Play
Willis Hall

Willis Hall began his writing career during military service when he was responsible for many scripts for Radio Malaya. After returning to England he had his first major success in the theatre with *The Long and the Short and the Tall*, which won him the *Evening Standard* 'Best Play of the Year' award in 1959. Since then, he has written many plays for the theatre, a number of them in collaboration with Keith Waterhouse, including *Billy Liar*, *Celebration*, *Say Who You Are*, etc. In addition to his work in the theatre, Willis Hall has written extensively for both the cinema and television. His TV plays include *The Villa Maroc*, *They Don't All Open Men's Boutiques* and *A Song At Twilight*. He has also written a number of children's books and plays including the *Kidnapped at Christmas* trilogy. He has an avid interest in sport in general and soccer in particular, and has written a number of books on sport as well as countless journalistic pieces.

1 The hopes I carried for my son's future as a sporting giant took another severe jolt last week when he set off for school carrying a large gold-and-off-white teddy bear. He is now coming up for seven, an age when I had expected him to go striding away with a pair of dinky soccer boots slung round his neck, or lugging a miniature   5 cricket bag.

2   Furthermore, he carried the teddy bear without embarrassment and without benefit of plain cover or carrier bag. His claim that his Junior Mixed Infants School was holding a Teddy Bear Week seemed scant excuse, and served only to strengthen my doubts about   10 modern education.

3   Surely, at coming up seven, Tom Brown was playing wing-three-quarter for Rugby's Second XV – to say nothing of being held over fires by older and wiser boys as part of a rigid toughening-up process? Even in these namby-pamby modern days, if I am to believe   15 my *Sunday Times*, Michael Parkinson has a whole host of sturdy sons who tuck home goals and know exactly where silly mid-off is situated.

4   Where did it all go wrong, I begin to wonder?

5   I set the lad off on the right foot, surely to Malcolm Allison? I   20 obtained the services of an ex-England soccer captain as his godfather. I obtained permission from a leading National Hunt

35

jockey to name the boy after him. I should explain, perhaps, that for many years I have cherished a fantasy in which I father a boy who rushes off the Wembley turf, having captained Leeds United to F A 25 Cup victory, nips into a waiting helicopter, and skies away to ride home the 33–1 outsider in the last race at Kempton. In my fantasy, the boy winks at his grizzled father on his way out of the paddock: 'Try me for a fiver each way, old 'un!' Thus had I dreamed of being kept in my old age. 30

6   Again, I ask myself, where did it all go wrong? To begin with, my aspirations for the lad's racing career took a steep nosedive when he began to experience serious problems with his racing weight at the age of two and a half. On top of which, his soccer future began to look less than rosy when the very sight of a blown-up football was 35 enough to send the lad into screaming tantrums.

7   When the boy was three, I put up a set of junior goal-posts in the garden to egg him along. Then, as he seemed to have no talent whatsoever for kicking the ball with either foot, let alone both, I engaged the help of a friendly ex-Fulham goalkeeper who agreed to 40 come round regularly and give him lessons between the sticks. The friendly ex-Fulham goalkeeper, being a good chum of the ex-England captain godfather to the boy, was full of enthusiasm at first, but gave up entirely halfway through the second session. My son, it seemed, had a rare gift for diving out of the way of the approaching 45 ball.

8   'I'm afraid he hasn't got it, Willis,' sighed my friendly ex-Fulham goalkeeper, and I have not set eyes on him from that day to this.

9   Not that I was deterred by early setbacks – and as witness to the fact, my cellar and summerhouse are both knee-deep in various 50 discarded sporting equipments in midget sizes: tiny tennis racquets plus balls and net; a half-set of golf clubs cut down to size; almost all of a kiddies' cricket outfit; shuttlecocks galore. There is even a miniature baseball bat, catcher's glove and Los Angeles Dodgers' cap, gifts from a kindly itinerant Hollywood restaurateur. My 55 garden resembles an Olympic training ground for dwarfs.

10   My son not only ignores this panoply of sporting opportunity – he will not even venture out of doors into God's good air except under threat of physical torture.

11   When he arrived at the ripe old age of six, I was ready to admit 60 defeat. After all, I am informed that Australian swimming champions are chucked into the deep end at the age of two – sink or swim. He had turned down my birthday offer of a matchball and a rowing machine in favour of an encyclopedia of prehistoric animals and a matched set of coloured ballpoints. And it was at this stage that my 65 mind began to think in other directions. Perhaps I was being too

harsh on him? For what was there in my own past sporting history for him to hook his personal star on? My four or five appearances for the regimental team in Singapore hardly qualified me for the Sportsman of the Year Award, *circa* 1953. And, if the lad did take *70* after me, why not capitalise on it? The pen is mightier than the vaulting pole, at least as far as raking in the shekels is concerned.

12   I arrived at a decision. If he was not cut out to be a Billy Bremner or a Norman Hunter or an Eddie Gray – why not a Hugh McIlvanney or a Geoffrey Green or a Brian Glanville? I immediately experienced *75* a new and pleasing fantasy:

'Hello, old'un! Sorry to ring you at this time of night, but I've got a couple of tickets going spare in the press-box for tomorrow's Wembley final. I'll leave them in our name at the ticket-office.'

13   Not at all a bad parental fantasy – for starters. But if my dream *80* was to become reality, I would have to backtrack slightly. I had got his back up about sport, and it was up to me to kindle in him a love of games. I decided upon a fatherly chat to begin with.

14   'Look here, son, if you've definitely decided against participating in competitive sport . . . ' His eyes lit up. I was off to a good start. 'I *85* honestly don't mind, but if you have definitely made your mind up that you're not going to take part yourself, why not start watching other people play football?'

'What for?' He found the idea novel if not intriguing.

'Well, now . . . ' I was patience itself. 'Lots of lads who don't *90* actually *play* themselves, go along to their local grounds and watch their favourite teams play on Saturday afternoons. Or, if they can't actually *go*, they read about them or watch them on the telly. They're called fans. You've seen them standing around football grounds on *The Big Match* every Sunday afternoon.' He seemed unsure, and so I *95* added as clarification: 'It comes on after *Thunderbirds*.'

'Oh, yes.' His brow cleared.

'So how about it?'

'Me?'

'Mmmm. Mmmmm. Certainly. I don't see why not.'   *100*

'What do I have to do?'

'Well – choose a team. Any team. And follow it.'

15   The above keen and intelligent sporting conversation was followed by a three day pause, after which he came up to me off his own bat and stated: *105*

'I'm Liverpool.'

'Good! Great!' I enthused. 'You'll like that. There's Kevin Keegan and Stevie Heighway and we'll look in the paper together, it's called the *Classified*, and see how they've got on and so forth. . . . '   *110*

16   Suddenly, it seemed, a great weight had been lifted from my shoulders – had some of it come to rest, I wondered, upon the able shoulders of Bill Shankly? I bought the boy a buttonhole badge and, the very next day, he set out for school displaying it, bravely.

17   He came home without it.   *115*

'What's happened to your Liverpool badge?'

'I'm not Liverpool any longer.'

'Why not?' I tried to keep calm.

'Because Harold Bullock, in my class, says Liverpool are crackers.'   *120*

'Well, Bill Shankly doesn't think so! And what about Stevie Heighway and Kevin Keegan?'

'I don't know.' He shrugged. 'Anyway, I'm not Liverpool any longer. I'm Leeds United.'

18   To be absolutely honest, my heart rose. I couldn't really fault the *125* lad for I have been a Leeds United supporter all my life. I bequeathed to him a buttonhole badge of my own and, to be fair to the lad, he wore it regularly.

19   A couple of months ago, I took him to see his first full ninety minutes of football. Not Leeds United, for we live in the South of *130* England, but the local amateur team of which I am club president. We stood on the terraces together, father and son, along with a couple of hundred other stalwarts. The lad watched the game for several minutes, then ventured:

'Which ones are Leeds United?'   *135*

'Neither. The ones in the blue-and-gold are St Albans and the ones in the white are Dulwich Hamlet.'

'Oh.'

20   As far as I could gather, the answer neither surprised nor displeased him. Neither did it seem to interest him greatly. Some *140* minutes later he drifted away from the terraces and spent the remainder of the first forty-five minutes throwing Coca-Cola bottle tops at the park railings. When I looked for him at half-time he had gone home. He has never mentioned St Albans City, Dulwich Hamlet, or even Leeds United again.   *145*

21   ˊSo where *did* I go wrong?

22   The lad comes from sturdy Yorkshire stock. Is there none of that county fire in his veins similar to that which courses through the veins of Freddie Trueman or Roger Taylor or Harvey Smith?

23   No – none. Well, perhaps there is still hope.   *150*

24   Last Friday, at the end of Teddy Bear Week at his Junior Mixed Infants School, my son came home lugging back his gold-and-off-white teddy bear. The bear was sporting a rosette, having been awarded, it read, 'Third Prize For Cheekiest Teddy'. Did I detect a

faint glimmer of triumph in the lad's eyes? I think I did.   *155*

25   Next year at this time he will be coming up for eight, and what then? 'Second Prize For Best Dressed Teddy'? And what about the year after that? 'First Prize – Best Teddy Overall'! It's possible.

26   Yes, there is hope still. So look out, you would be Olympians for 1984. We Halls are notoriously slow-starters but when the chips are *160* down . . .

From *Football Classified: An Anthology of Soccer*

1   **a**   'Where did it all go wrong?' *(line 19)*

    (i) What **assumption** lies behind this question?
    (ii) What is your answer to the question?

  b   Willis Hall's hopes for his son lay in two main directions.

    (i) What were they and why were the hopes disappointed?
    (ii) How are the two 'parental fantasies' *(lines 24 and 80)* related to (i) above?
    (iii) What parental fantasy seems to be **implied** at the end of the passage?

  c   What career fantasies, sporting or other, have you entertained?

  d   Say or guess what the following have to do with sport:

Kempton *(line 27)*, Norman Hunter *(line 74)*, Brian Glanville *(line 75)*, Stevie Heighway *(line 108)*, Bill Shankly *(line 113)*, Harvey Smith *(line 149)*.

2   **a**   The humour of the piece often depends on picking up this writer's clues or filling out his hints. How might this be done for:

    (i) 'without benefit of plain cover' *(line 8)*
    (ii) 'Rugby's Second XV' *(line 13)*
    (iii) 'being kept in my old age' *(lines 29–30)*
    (iv) 'a rare gift' *(line 45)*
    (v) 'the pen is mightier than the vaulting pole' *(lines 71–72)*
    (vi) 'His eyes lit up' *(line 85)*
    (vii) 'Mmmm. Mmmmm.' *(line 100)*
    (viii) 'a couple of hundred other stalwarts' *(lines 132–3)*
    (ix) 'So where *did* I go wrong?' *(line 146)*

(x) 'a faint glimmer of triumph in the lad's eyes' *(lines 154—155)*?

b Exaggeration or **hyperbole** also adds to the humour, e.g. 'held over fires' *(lines 13—14)* 'serious problems with his racing weight at the age of two and a half' *(lines 33—34)*.

Can you find four similar examples?

c The humorous **tone** is also suggested by such **stylistic** features as:

(i) **formal register** used for a trivial event
(ii) **understatement**
(iii) **irony**
(iv) **anticlimax** or **bathos**
(v) **formal** and **informal** registers in **juxtaposition**.

Say which one or more of the above is exemplified by each of these:

(vi) 'my aspirations . . . a steep nosedive' *(lines 31—32)*
(vii) 'hardly qualified me' *(line 69)*
(viii) 'keen and intelligent sporting conversation' *(line 103)*
(ix) 'bequeathed' *(line 126)*
(x) 'Third Prize for Cheekiest Teddy' *(line 154)*.

3 Imagine that the father's hope for 1984 was realised but in some way proved more than he bargained for. Write his reflections in a few paragraphs.

11 The Occupational Culture of the Boxer

S. K. Weinberg and H. Arond

'What contributions are made by sports and games to the life of the individual and to the society of which he is a member?' This is one of the questions posed by Eric Dunning, Lecturer in Sociology at Leicester University, in his introduction to *The Sociology of Sport*, a collection of papers ranging from 'The Play Element in Contemporary Sports' to 'Football Hooliganism'. The essay on the boxer was based on research and interviews with sixty-eight boxers, seven trainers and five managers.

1　The boxer comes to regard his body, especially his hands, as his stock-in-trade. Boxers have varied formulas for preventing their hands from excess swelling, from excessive pain, or from being broken. This does not mean a hypochondriacal interest, because they emphasise virility and learn to slough off and to disdain　5 punishment. But fighters continually seek nostrums and exercises for improving their bodies. One practised Yoga, another became a physical cultist, a third went on periodic fasts; others seek out lotions, vitamins, and other means of improving their endurance, alertness, and punching power.　10

2　'You have to live up to being a fighter.' This phrase justifies their deprivations and regulated living. There is also a cult of a kind of persevering courage, called a 'fighting heart', which means 'never admitting defeat'. The fighter learns early that his exhibited courage – his ability, if necessary, to go down fighting – charac-　15 terises the respected, audience-pleasing boxer. He must cherish the lingering hope that he can win by a few more punches. One fighter was so severely beaten by another that the referee stopped the bout. The brother of the beaten fighter, a former fighter himself, became so outraged that he climbed into the ring and started to brawl with the　20 referee. In another instance a boxer incurred a very severe eye injury, which would have meant the loss of his sight. But he insisted on continuing to fight, despite the warnings of his seconds. When the fight was stopped, he protested. This common attitude among boxers is reinforced by the demands of the spectators, who generally　25 cheer a 'game fighter'. Thus the beaten fighter may become a 'crowd-pleaser' and may get matches despite his defeat. On the other hand, some fighters who are influenced by friends, by wives, or by sheer experience recognise that sustained beatings may leave permanent injuries and voluntarily quit when they are beaten. But the spirit of 30 the code is that the boxer continue to fight regardless of injuries. 'If a man quits a fight, an honest fight,' claimed one fighter, 'he has no business there in the first place.'

3   Fighters who remain in the sport are always hopeful of occupational climbing. This attitude may initially be due to a definite self- 35 centredness, but it is intensified by the character of boxing. Boxing is done by single contestants, not by teams. Emphasis is on the boxer as a distinct individual. The mores among boxers are such that fighters seldom admit to others that they are 'punchy' or 'washed-up'. One fighter said 'You can tell another fighter to quit, but you can't call 40 him punchy. If you do, he'll punch you to show you he still has a punch.' He has to keep up his front.

4   Further, the boxer is involved in a scheme of relationships and traditions which focus upon building confidence. The boxing tradition is full of legends of feats of exceptional fighters. Most 45 gymnasiums have pictures of past and present outstanding boxers on the wall, and identification with them comes easy for the incoming fighters. Past fights are revived in tales. Exceptional fighters of the past and present are compared and appraised. Second, the individual boxer is continually assured and reassured that he is 'great' and that 50 he is 'coming up'. As a result, many fighters seem to overrate their ability and to feel that all they need are 'lucky breaks' to become champions or leading contenders. Many get self-important and carry scrapbooks of their newspaper write-ups and pictures.

5   The process of stimulating morale among fighters is an integral 55 accompaniment of the acquisition of boxing skills and body conditioning. The exceptions are the part-time fighters who hold outside jobs and who are in the preliminary ranks. They tend to remain on the periphery of the boxing culture and thus have a somewhat different perspective on the mobility aspects of the sport. 60

6   Since most bouts are unpredictable, boxers usually have superstitions which serve to create confidence and emotional security among them. Sometimes the manager or trainer uses these superstitions to control the fighter. One fighter believed that, if he ate certain foods, he was sure to win, because these foods gave him 65 strength. Others insist on wearing the same robe in which they won their first fight: one wore an Indian blanket when he entered the ring. Many have charm pieces or attribute added importance to entering the ring after the opponent. Joe Louis insisted on using a certain dressing-room at Madison Square Garden. Some insist that, if a 70

woman watches them train, it is bad luck. One fighter, to show he was not superstitious, would walk under a ladder before every fight, until this became a magical rite itself. Consistent with this attitude, many intensify their religious attitudes and keep Bibles in their lockers. One fighter kept a rosary in his glove. If he lost the rosary, he *75* would spend the morning before the fight in church. Although this superstitious attitude may be imported from local or ethnic culture, it is intensified among the boxers themselves, whether they are white or Negro, preliminary fighters or champions.

7   When a fighter likes the style, punch, or movement of another *80* fighter, he may wear the latter's trunks or one of his socks or rub him on the back. In training camps some fighters make a point of sleeping in the bed that a champion once occupied. For this reason, in part, some take the names of former fighters. All these practices focus towards the perspective of 'filling the place' or taking the role of the *85* other esteemed fighter. Moreover, many fighters deliberately copy the modes of training, the style, and the general movements of role-models.

8   Since fighters, in the process of training, become keyed to a finely balanced physical and emotional condition and frequently are *90* irritable, restless, and anxious, they also grow dependent and suggestible. The superstitions and the reassuring statements of the trainer and manager both unwittingly and wittingly serve to bolster their confidence.

9   Before and during the bout, self-confidence is essential. Fighters *95* or their seconds try to unnerve the opponent. They may try to outstare him or make some irritating or deflating remarks or gestures. In the ring, tactical self-confidence is expressed in the boxer's general physical condition and movements. His ability to outslug, to outspar, or to absorb punishment is part of his morale. *100* The ability not to go down, to out-manoeuvre the other contestant, to change his style in whole or in part, to retrieve his strength quickly, or to place the opponent off-balance inevitably affect the latter's confidence. A fighter can feel whether he will win a bout during the early rounds, but he is always wary of the dreaded single punch or *105* the unexpected rally.

10   Boxers become typed by their style and manner in the ring. A 'puncher' or 'mauler' differs from a 'boxer' and certainly from a 'cream puff', who is unable to hit hard. A 'miller', or continual swinger, differs from one who saves his energy by fewer movements. *110* A 'butcher' is recognised by his tendency to hit hard and ruthlessly when another boxer is helpless, inflicting needless damage. A 'tanker' is one who goes down easily, sometimes in a fixed fight or 'set-up'. The 'mechanical' fighter differs from the 'smart' fighter, for

among the 'smart' fighters are really the esteemed fighters, those who *115*
are capable of improvising and reformulating their styles, or devising
original punches and leg movements, of cunningly outmanoeuvering
their opponents, and of possessing the compensatory hostility,
deadly impulsiveness, and quick reflexes to finish off their opponents
in the vital split second.   *120*

11   Boxers have to contend with fouls and quasi-fouls in the ring. At
present, these tactics seemingly are becoming more frequent. They
may have to contend with 'heeling', the manœuvre by which the
fighter, during clinches, shoves the laced part of his glove over the
opponent's wound, particularly an 'eye' wound, to open or *125*
exacerbate it, with 'thumbing' in the eye, with 'butting' by the head,
with having their insteps stepped on hard during clinches, with
punches in back of the head or in the kidneys, or with being tripped.
These tactics, which technically are fouls, may be executed so quickly
and so cleverly that the referee does not detect them. When detected, *130*
the fighter may be warned or, at worst, may lose the round. The
boxers are thus placed in a situation fraught with tension, physical
punishment, and eventual fatigue. They may be harassed by the
spectators. Their protection consists of their physical condition and
their acquired confidence. Moreover, the outcome of the fight is *135*
decisive for their status and self-esteem.

From *The Sociology of Sport*

---

1 a Which of these would make the best sub-title for the extract?

    (i) Boxers past and present
    (ii) The advantages and disadvantages of boxing
    (iii) How the boxer boosts his morale
    (iv) Is boxing a sport?

  b (i) Rearrange the following to make a brief **summary** of
       paragraphs 1–6:

    A They compete as individuals.
    B Professionals, however, adopt all sorts of superstitious
       practices to bolster morale.
    C They also have to cultivate an attitude of toughness and
       courage even in the face of severe punishment.
    D Boxers have a constant concern to maintain body fitness.

E Fringe boxers are less dependent on these things.

F To boost their ego they identify with past heroes and seek constant reassurance about their prowess.

(ii) Summarise paragraphs 7–11 in the same way.

c Is the authors' attitude to boxing critical, sympathetic or objective?

d What in your opinion are the three main problems of the boxer, as suggested by the passage?

e Say why you would or would not wish to be a successful boxer.

2 a What points in the **context** of these words help to suggest or confirm their meaning:

'hypochondriacal' *(line 4)* 'nostrums' *(line 6)* 'cultist' *(line 8)* 'deprivations' *(line 12)* 'mores' *(line 38)* 'periphery' *(line 59)* 'rosary' *(line 75)* 'ethnic' *(line 77)* 'quasi-' *(line 121)* 'exacerbate' *(line 126)*?

b How would you distinguish between confidence, status and self-esteem *(lines 135–136)*?

c Some of the words in inverted commas in paragraphs 10 and 11 could be called **slang**, others **jargon**. Choose two for each category, giving reasons for your choice.

d List five slang and five jargon terms not in the passage, giving their meaning and saying what sphere of life they come from.

3 a Consider the word 'culture' in the title and in lines 59 and 77, and attempt a general **definition** of it.

b Boxing has been criticised as a brutal sport for both participants and spectators. Suggest arguments for and/or against this opinion.

c Suppose that the sociologists who wrote this piece decided to investigate football or some other sport. Devise:

(i) Five questions they might seek to answer by general research

(ii) Five questions they might include on a questionnaire for participants.

12 Life Really Starts When I Push That Button

Alistair MacLean

The extract is from 'Racing Fever', a contribution by Alistair MacLean (whose novel *The Way to Dusty Death* includes a thrilling motor-race) to a collection of essays on Jackie Stewart. They cover his career and track-record as a racing driver, his personality, his family and his own thoughts on the sport in which he excelled.

1 I have been to Formula One Grand Prix races but make no claim to being a devoted *aficionado*. Whether this necessarily leads to a detached viewpoint or a properly judicial consideration, I do not know. I just know that I am not conscious of any deep involvement.

2   That there are those who turn up at the Grand Prix tracks of the   *5* world in the anticipation of seeing a racing car crash into a wall – or better still into another car – at speeds of anything up to 200 miles per hour, with the concomitant bursting of fuel tanks and blazing white flames from the magnesium alloy wheels, I do not for a moment doubt. If a driver is killed or burnt to death, all the better *10* reason for the arms to be held high in hypocritical horror – and it is an unfortunate fact that occasions for the expression of this horror occur with dismaying frequency.

3   For the dedicated ghoul, the opportunities for the expression of his blood-lust come in an endless variety of permutations, ranging *15* from a pleasantly spine-chilling thrill when a car goes into a dangerous skid to a kind of inverted religious ecstasy when the zenith of his twisted ambitions has been realized in a multiple pile-up from which, preferably, no one emerges unscathed.

4   I have known, slightly, a few racing drivers – one well enough to *20* call a friend – and they are unanimous in their opinion that such a maniacal element does exist. As those most intimately concerned, they are singularly unappreciative of his attitude of mind. This *morituri te salutamus* syndrome has no appeal of any kind for them. They do not visualize themselves in the roles of latter-day gladiators, *25* using enormously horse-powered cars for weapons instead of sword, net and trident for the edification of a Roman bread-and-circuses mob. Each of them wants just to be first past the finishing post –

without, if possible, so much as scratching his own paint, or that of any of his competitors.   *30*

5   Statistics, of course, are impossible to come by. Few, if any, of us are possessed of Uri Geller's alleged ability to read minds but those same drivers are convinced that the sadistic element constitutes only a tiny fraction of the viewing public. I am sure they are right, and that the hypnotic attraction of motor racing – especially Grand Prix *35* racing – lies elsewhere.

6   A Grand Prix driver once said to me: 'I have a beautiful wife, beautiful children and a beautiful home' – and he unquestionably has all of those – 'but life really starts for me when I push that button.' I doubt whether he still holds that view, but I do not doubt *40* that he meant it at the time he said it.

7   For this is where the greatest appeal of motor racing lies. It brings out a greater degree of audience participation and total involvement than any other sport I know. Life also starts for the crowd when that button is pressed. In fact, it is they who press the button, for it is in *45* this admittedly highly dangerous but indisputably glamorous sport that Walter Mitty comes into his own. Here hero-worship reaches its summit, a totally committed empathy its peak.

8   The Stewarts, the Hills, the Fittipaldis may believe they are driving alone, but they couldn't be further wrong. Each is accompanied by *50* thousands of devoted and concerned co-drivers – no small feat, granted, in a tailor-made cockpit – who change gears whenever he changes gears, brake when he brakes, overtake when he overtakes and help him corner to the limit of adhesion. Many of the more critically minded co-drivers are probably of the opinion that they *55* could do better themselves, but that does not alter their worshipful admiration of the young and sometimes not-so-young – *pace* Graham Hill – demi-gods behind the wheel. They're with him there all the way, never more so than during those nail-biting moments when he's out of sight on the other side of the course. Far from any *60* blood-lust being in his mind, the co-driver devoutly wishes him well. For he's in that car too.

9   Next in importance to the participation factor is the one of competition. Competition, after all, is the *raison d'être* of sport. Crowds don't jam football stadiums in the hope of witnessing a *65* blood-bath. Although a miniscule section may be incurable hoodlums, their minds are not necessarily filled with the longing for blood; they are just bloody-minded, which is a different thing entirely. They are there for the competition. Rod Laver and John Newcombe do not regard the tennis court as a jousting ground where *70* honour demands that they belabour each other over their heads with a tennis racket: they go out to compete. Spassky and Fischer have

never – to the best of my knowledge – been known to hurl chessmen at each other, but they held much of the civilised world spellbound during their world championship encounter in Iceland. They were – *75* all too obviously – just competing.

10   And there cannot be a more demandingly competitive sport in the world than motor racing. It *is* the most competitive sport in the world. In most other sports, one has either team versus team or individual versus individual. Here every individual is up against *80* every other individual, with the result that one does not have just one contest but many contests. The dicing between cars lying seventh and eighth may be just as enthralling as the duel for first place. And in no other sports do fortunes change so rapidly, with advantages being gained and lost with such bewildering speed, and to the *85* accompaniment of an almost unbearable tension and excitement.

11   Inseparable from the competitive element is that of skill. As with the first two factors, here motor racing surely stands alone. There are many excellent footballers, cricket players, basketball players and players in a dozen other sports in the world, but there are not many *90* excellent racing drivers. Though there may be anything up to twenty-four Formula One Grand Prix drivers, the truly great ones can be counted on one's fingers – and if one were to lose the odd finger or thumb the assertion would still stand. Those few drive their machines – and themselves – to the utter limit, where a fraction *95* error, a tiny percentage in judgment can quite literally mark that shadowy boundary between life and death.

12   The closest one can get to this factor of icecold judgment is to see a Mike Hailwood lean his motor bike over to an amazing angle of fifty-seven degrees as he rounds a corner. But somehow motor *100* cycling does not command the immense public following that motor racing does. In any event, all we can do is watch in sad envy, knowing that it is a capacity that will forever lie beyond our reach, our immortals of the sport displaying skills that border on the supernatural. *105*

13   Then, of course, comes the factor of sheer speed. The spectacle of a Grand Prix car passing in a blinding blur as it hurtles along the long straight at Le Mans at something in excess of 200 miles per hour cannot fail to stir even the most blasé. Speed has always fascinated man – and motor racing is the fastest sport on earth. *110*

14   All those elements – involvement, competition, skill and speed – are essential to the understanding of racing fever, because in no other sport are any of the four so splendidly exemplified. But there are three other factors that contribute to motor racing's pre-eminence among sports. *115*

15   There is the factor of noise. The shattering roar of an eight-

cyclinder Ford-Cosworth engine accelerating up to maximum revolutions is an auditory experience never to be forgotten, especially when it is accompanied by the screaming of tyres as the sliding car comes out of a corner. There is the unmistakable smell of *120* hot oil, of burnt high octane fuel, of burnt rubber and dust. And, always, there is the roar of the crowd. To all of those things the vast majority of racing enthusiasts become quickly and permanently addicted.

16 I think the word 'addiction' sums it up. Grand Prix motor racing is *125* concerned with the blood all right, but not with blood-lust: it is a disease of the blood for which there appears to be no known cure.

From *The exciting World of Jackie Stewart*

1 a How would you differentiate between sports, games and pastimes?

   b (i) The word *'aficionado'* *(line 2)* suggests a comparison between motor-racing and bullfighting. Say what the two sports have and have not in common.
      (ii) If one of the two sports had to be abolished, say which you think it should be and why.

   c (i) Say what the following phrases have in common and
      (ii) explain the **allusions** contained in *two* of them:

      A 'hypocritical horror' *(line 11)*
      B 'dedicated ghoul' *(line 14)*
      C 'maniacal element' *(line 22)*
      D 'a Roman bread-and-circuses mob' *(lines 27–28)*
      E 'the sadistic element' *(line 33)*.

2 a There might seem to be a **contradiction** between the last sentence of paragraph 4 and the first of paragraph 6. Say if and why you think there is or is not.

   b The end of paragraph 8 and the whole of paragraph 14 are important points in the **cohesive** structure of the passage. Show why this is so.

c (i) The following chart shows factors in the appeal of various sports. Complete it, using a six-point scale (5 = high; O = nil) to show your estimate of the factors involved.

	Audience involvement	Competition	Skill	Speed	List other factors
A. Motor racing: Author's opinion:	5	5	5	5	Noise of cars, smell, crowd roar
Your opinion:					
B. Soccer					
C. Ice hockey					
D. Mountaineering					
E. Squash					
F. (Others)					

(ii) The author **cites** various sportsmen to **exemplify** certain points. How many of these are in motor racing; how many in other sports?

(iii) Provide **examples** of various kinds, including sportsmen and women, to illustrate five of the scores in your chart in (i).

d Consider lines 122–127 and say with reasons if you think the word 'addiction' is a **metaphor**.

e In what respects is the passage

(i) argumentative, (ii) critical, (iii) imaginative?

3 a Visitors from the eighteenth and twenty-eighth centuries arrive by Time Machine at a motor race. Give the reactions of one or both of them.

b The author thinks that motor-racing drivers have 'skills that border on the supernatural'. Describe a sports scene where a participant suddenly acquires supernatural skills.

13 Seaside Holiday

Anthony Hern

Anthony Hern finished, in 1980, a twenty-year stint as Literary Editor of the *Evening Standard* in London: the latest in a series of newspaper jobs which began when he left Farnham Grammar School, as it then was, to become an apprenticed reporter on a local paper. Unashamed curiosity about people has kept him busy since then. He is the author of countless newspaper and periodical articles – 'countless' because he hasn't kept a record – and is adding to the total by writing pieces about wine.

1 With a £500 half-page advertisement in the *Daily Express*, Butlin announced his scheme for the spring of 1936. The initial response, booking chalets with a ten-shilling registration fee, was overwhelming. Long before the camp was ready, long before even the site had a guaranteed water supply, the chalets were practically booked 5 solid for the whole of the following season.

2 Yet it nearly went wrong.

3 The holidaymakers turned up as booked that very first week. But they didn't *do* anything. They sat around the bathing pool or the boating lake; they seemed to enjoy their food in the big restaurant; 10 but there was a rather chilling silence over the place. What had happened was that they were bored. As a family group they probably would not have been, or at least they would not have been noticed. But as groups or individuals in a crowd it was clear they were all uneasy. There was the crowd, but it didn't feel like a holiday crowd: 15 there was no mateyness, no communal laughter in the communal café. Perhaps there shouldn't have been. There is no recipe for instant jolliness.

4 At Butlin's Luxury Holiday Camp, the 'campers' arrived as individuals but were expecting or at least hoping to be absorbed into 20 a communal movement of pleasure. And nothing had happened. Butlin, with his showman's instinct for an audience he was losing, was worried. Bored holidaymakers were going to be no advertisement for the Butlin Idea. 'What's wrong with them?' he is said to have asked his aides. Someone suggested they were lonely, and that 25 was why they had come to a camp: to shrug off loneliness, and no one was helping them. One of the aides, Mr Norman Bradford, went to

51

the dining room microphone installed to make announcements and
began to tell jokes. It sounds dreadful, but it worked. People
laughed. Boredom vanished. Butlin saw that something like this had *30*
to be a permanent part of the camp atmosphere. He told Bradford to
wear a bright-coloured blazer and be in front of that microphone
next morning belting out cheery greetings. That sounds even more
dreadful. But it too worked. Everyone had a wonderful time for the
rest of the week, and Butlin's Redcoats were in business. *35*

5   They personalise the idea of a Holiday Camp so exactly that they
represent to the enthusiastic holiday-camper exactly what he would
miss if he went to lodgings or a boarding house, and to the
individualist holiday-maker exactly what he most dislikes about the
idea of a holiday camp. The bifurcation of the English holiday *40*
habit – with one sort of holidaymaker gravitating towards the
crowded beaches and having a riotous holiday and another sort
seeking with intensity the remotest cove in the farthest part of
Cornwall and thoroughly enjoying the resultant peace – has never
been more sharply delineated than by Billy Butlin that year in *45*
Skegness. From the start you either hated the very idea of a holiday
camp; or you said: 'One day we'll give it a try.' Millions have done
either; but no one has done both.

6   The standard Butlinesque explanation for the 'socially significant'
success of the Holiday Camps and the ancillary Redcoats is that *50*
'holidaymakers are more relaxed if relieved of some thinking and
organising. Throughout the year, most of them work hard for a boss.
One elementary reason for the success of a Butlin camp is that Big
Boss Butlin is working for the holidaymaker by providing
everything . . . which they can take or leave.' *55*

7   Redcoats do not, according to the Butlin brief, attempt to
regiment customers into some kind of fun factory (even though to an
unsympathetic or quizzical onlooker it must sometimes seem like
that). They do lead, advise, explain, comfort, help out and generally,
in the words of Rex North, 'make themselves the closest thing to *60*
holiday angels on earth'.

8   The theory that because people are accustomed by economic
necessity to take orders in a working week, they therefore become
acclimatised or indoctrinated to accept orders even on holiday is a
pessimistically mechanistic one; and indeed is not borne out by some *65*
of the Class A exhibits quoted by the Butlin publicity office.

From *The Seaside Holiday*

1 a What, in the author's view, would a holiday-camper 'miss if he went to a lodgings or boarding house' *(line 38)*?

  b What would the 'other sort' of holiday-maker want?

  c The author's **tone** suggests a slightly mocking attitude about both types of holiday. Quote two phrases to show this.

  d As a 'Class A exhibit' *(line 66)* the writer goes on to mention a 'middle-class lady in her sixties' who went to the Butlin Holiday Camp at Skegness. Deduce what sort of experiences she had there.

2 a 'Communal' *(lines 16 and 21)*, 'individualist' *(line 39)* and 'bifurcation' *(line 40)* are key words in the first part *(paragraphs 1–5)* of the passage. Say why.

  b What does 'socially significant' *(line 49)* mean? Why is the expression in inverted commas?

  c What words in lines 50–64 correspond to these meanings:

  (i) financial (ii) coerce (iii) auxiliary (iv) brainwashed (v) sceptical (vi) habituated (vii) simple (viii) hypothesis?

  d The 'theory' explained in paragraph 8 refers back to ideas in the two previous paragraphs. Explain the connection.

  e The shortest sentences in the extract contain five words or fewer, the longest over fifty. Choose two short and two long sentences and say what effect is achieved by the length of sentence in each case.

3 a Later in this chapter Anthony Hern mentions other features of Butlin's Holiday Camps:

  shows, concert parties, swimming, tennis, quoits, pingpong, dancing, knobbly knees contests, sandpits for children, free movies, fancy-dress balls, canned music, private chalets, coarse jokes.

  Write a humorous dialogue referring to some of these.

  b List ten ingredients of your ideal holiday.

14 Life in the Year AD 2000

Colin Leicester

The book in which the extract by Colin Leicester is included is a collection of pieces concerned with what cities might or should be like in the future, ranging from More's *Utopia* to contemporary town planning and the anti-Utopias of Huxley and Orwell.

———————

1 *Date-line: 1 May 2000 AD*
7.00 a.m. Somewhere in the megalopolis of Manbirlon, which cuts a built-up swathe across Britain from merseyside to thameside, Everybrit (the average Briton), awakes from a controlled sleep. Over his underwear made from paper, he pulls a synthetic outer garment, temperature-regulated and powered by a tiny fuel cell. As he begins a   5
breakfast of synthetic proteins, one complete wall of the living room flickers into coloured, three-dimensional, televisual life. The newscast that morning contained another report from the second manned expedition to Mars, a film of the United Nations patrol taking fresh stock from coastal hatcheries to the Dogger Bank fish-farms, and an   10
urgent statement from the International Weather Bureau's network of communication satellites and deep ocean buoys: fast ATOL and VTOL aircraft were speeding with loads of an organic salt of magnesium into the Western Pacific to quell an incipient hurricane.
2   8.00 a.m. Breakfast over, Everybrit attends to some private   15
matters. At the electronic console in the living room, he dials for all the sporting sections of the local newspapers; and while they are being printed, he does a week's shopping. The catalogues of retail warehouses flash onto the visual display screen. Every item is a mass-produced, standardised good, well-packaged for convenience, hy-   20
giene and for transportation by underground conveyor to his cellar; but each category of goods is a variety of brands and styles from all over the globe. He quantifies his demands, adding Japanese oysters as an afterthought. His order, like countless others, has two repercussions: his bank account is automatically debited, and the   25
information of the sale has passed back from retailer to manufacturer to supplier of raw materials via an automatic system of inventory control and production scheduling. Musing over the high-efficiency, integrated economy in which he works, Everybrit dials the

central library and checks his memory of a quotation from an old, *30* venerated economic philosopher; and the display screen then reads –

3   ' . . . thus for the first time since his creation man will be faced with his real, his permanent problem – how to use his freedom from pressing economic cares, how to occupy his leisure, which science and compound interest will have won for him, to live wisely and *35* agreeably and well . . .'   (Keynes, 1931)

4   Keynes, thinks Everybrit to himself, was partly right after all. This being his last thirty-hour working week of his ten-month working year, Everybrit checks his reservation for a month's holiday in the *40* underwater oceanic resort of Atlantis: it is in order, and his custom-built submersible is promised for delivery at the same time. Finally, he calls for a list of the day's political issues and votes on them, sometimes making reference to the aggregate economic and social statistics of the population of Britain. Somewhere in the central *45* computerised databank of what was still nostalgically called Whitehall, there is a dossier containing all the legal, medical and social details of himself; it had formed a minute part of the information he had just used. Exercising his civil right, Everybrit demanded via the console to know if this personal dossier had been *50* opened by anybody during the last seven days. The answer was reassuring: no one.

5   9.00 a.m. Walking into his office next door, Everybrit notices that letters have already arrived by light-pipe. Printing them out, he reads his correspondence; dictates replies into a phonetic typewriter; *55* makes one or two minor revisions which the machine immediately duplicates; and despatches the finished copy by light-pipe. Letters received and sent are mechanically recorded and filed.

6   10.00 a.m. A conference of the technical directors from all subsidiaries of the firm has been arranged. The on-light of the visual *60* telephone winks; five screens light up; and Everybrit pushes the encoding button to ensure that, at least, his part of the six-man conversation will remain a business secret. The South-American opens the discussion, describing the simulation results of marketing the new multi-purpose synthetic material under different *65* assumptions, his lips out of synchronism with the voice of the automatic translator. The Frenchman interjects a series of questions; the American makes a blunt remark; Everybrit concurs. At a later stage, the matter is decided.

7   11.00 a.m. Everybrit leaves home. The weather forecast was spot *70* on again, he notes. No sooner is he out of the door, than a domestic robot trundles out of the cupboard under the stairs and performs its

55

chores, beginning by clearing up the breakfast table. Everybrit makes a mental note to change the structure and configuration of the living-room at the end of the week. He hops nimbly into the vehicle *75* outside, his cyborg legs appearing to any bystander no different from the real legs he lost in an accident thirty years ago in an ill-famed motorway pile-up. Once inside the hovercar, he presses a button and the machine rises on its cushion of air. He presses another, and the control system engages with the cybernated traffic control network. *80* He dials his destination (the air-city of Foulness) and already, he knows, the least congested route is being selected for him by the control network. The electric motor moves the hovercar onto the highway, scanning devices altering speed persistently to keep the vehicle a safe distance from all other vehicles. And Everybrit leans *85* back in his seat, reads the sports news, thinks ahead to his thirty-minute transoceanic flight by rocket jet to visit a new factory installation at Boswash on the eastern seaboard of the US. Taking hovercar, rather than hovertrain, to Foulness would allow him time to read the documents he had brought. Time, also, to think ahead to *90* this evening, when on return he would play tennis with a blind friend, sight-provided by radar spectacles. Perhaps, after that, he would visit the fun laboratory. The last thoughts Everybrit had, before he turned to his technical documents, were non-sequiturs. They were: 'shall I decide to have a girl as my next child?' . . . 'what paintings *95* would I be painting in the last part of my two-month holiday?' . . . and 'what shall I choose to study in the sabbatical year following?'

From *The Future Of Cities* (1970)

―――――

1   a   (i) What must we know to appreciate these details in Colin Leicester's account:

'Manbirlon' *(line 1)* and 'Boswash' *(line 88)*
'the United Nations Patrol' *(line 9)*
'what was still nostalgically called Whitehall' *(lines 46–47)*?

(ii) Mention three other points where a knowledge of the present is helpful.

b   What other 'real, permanent problems' than that mentioned by Keynes *(lines 32–36)* face man at present and in the future?

c Students of linguistics might say that an 'automatic translator' *(line 67)* was impossible. Say with reasons if you agree.

d The author's forecast was made some years ago. Choose five items from his picture and place them on a scale ranging from 'Already achieved' to 'Possible in the distant future'.

2 Say with reasons which one or more of these terms you would apply to the passage:
argumentative, impartial, prophetic, critical, humorous, rhetorical, visionary, speculative.

3 a How might Everybrit pass the time at the 'fun laboratory' *(line 93)*?

b Describe a few hours in the life of Everybrit's wife or female companion.

c Which features of this sketch of the future give grounds for optimism, which for pessimism?

15 Notes on a War
Kenneth Allsop

Kenneth Allsop was a journalist and TV interviewer and presenter. He was particularly interested in literature – *The Angry Decade* (1969) is a survey of the cultural revolt of the Fifties – and in nature. His book *In the Country* was published in 1972 and Allsop is remembered for his concern for wild life conservation.

1 My father was a 1914–18 front-line soldier. Had he been an archer at Agincourt, it couldn't have been remoter to me – this carnage on the wet Flanders plain that ended only a few years before my birth. Yet the battle-names I first heard from him, Arras and the Somme, Vimy Ridge and Passchendaele, hung in my head sombre as gunsmoke. *5*
2 And what speared me most was a song from the trenches, a parody of mocking melancholy. 'If you want the old battalion', it said, with brutal poignancy, 'I know where it is'.

'It's hanging on the old barbed wire.
I've seen 'em, I've seen 'em. *10*
Hanging on the old barbed wire.'

3 It haunted my childhood. Even then I felt its terrible irony and resignation, the imminence of mass scarecrow death on the desolation of no-man's-land faced with a phlegmatic realism beyond anguish. *15*
4 It has never ceased to haunt me – nor, I believe, all those of the generations born since it was over, even though other wars have intervened and now the Bomb in minutes could deal ten times the destruction so painfully and sweatily compiled during the Western Front four years. *20*
5 Joan Littlewood's shattering *Oh What a Lovely War* eerily recaptured the dazed chirrupyness with which Europe bled to death. Soon after came the BBC's stupendous twenty-six-programme documentary. And, half-a-century distant, the books still rake through the rubble with horrified fascination. *25*
6 Following the great written barrage of the twenties, the bitter

aftermath in which such ex-soldiers as Robert Graves, Siegfried Sassoon, Henry Williamson and Henri Barbusse cried the truth aloud, came a pause – then the rush of World War Two literature. It was merely a lull. Excluding biography and fiction like Williamson's *Chronicle of Ancient Sunlight* sequence and John Harris's *Covenant with Death*, more than forty reappraisals of 1914–18 campaigns and generalship have been published since 1956. There is no sign of the torrent ebbing.

7   What is insistently striking is that almost all the new wave authors – for instance, Alan Clark (*The Donkeys*), John Terraine (*Haig: The Educated Soldier*), Barry Pitt (*1918: The Last Act*) and Alistair Horne (*The Price of Glory*) are young men who served in 1939–45 or later, but who have been drawn back to tunnel into the boneyards of those battlefields where corn and woodlands again grow.

8   How can it be accounted for, this picking at the old wound, the fixed stare backward at ghosts?

9   When her *August 1914* appeared, Barbara W. Tuchman, the American historian, said: 'That was the birthday of us all. It was the chasm between the nineteenth-century world and our world.'

10   Perhaps it explains its grasp on our thoughts – in the then unborn a nostalgia for a security never known, in the survivors the sense of waste and sin. For World War One was a modern man's fall from innocence. Whistling a music hall song, he marched jauntily into the pit.

11   After the 1910 funeral of Edward VII, 'the Peacemaker', Lord Esher wrote: 'There never was such a break-up. All the old buoys who have marked the channel of our lives seem swept away.'

12   That was the overture. The tragedy was still to be enacted. It opened, as rehearsed for years, with all the great armies, glittering and arrogant, taking up their ordained positions for the tourney.

13   Ten million men had died before anyone found out how to stop what had begun so flippantly and bumptiously, and turned into something so unbelievably horrible.

14   Today, fifty years later, the depletion remains in our lives – the loss of a European generation, the loss of standards and order and faith that once seemed eternally rooted. The men trapped in it, those not left hanging on the old barbed wire, ever after felt isolated by an experience they could not adequately communicate.

15   So still we try to discover how – and why – men endured what they did, how others, their rulers and commanders, could have been both so wrong and so self-righteous.

16   For when in 1960 American military researchers fed into computers all the facts of World War One the machines whirred their

bafflement and returned the result that it couldn't have happened –
there couldn't have been so many blunders, so many fallen.

From *Scan*

1 a Paragraph 8 marks a turning point in the passage. Say why.

   b (i) What story is **alluded** to in paragraph 10?
      (ii) What have 'security', 'waste' and 'sin' to do with the story?
      (iii) How are these three points brought into paragraphs 13–15?

2   The passage contains some interesting **imagery**, especially
      metaphors. Say which *five* of these you think most effective, with
      reasons in the case of two of them.

3 a Why, in your view, does World War One seem to interest the
      present generation more than World War Two?

   b Write a dialogue between two civilians or two soldiers, one from
      each war. Some library research may help you with factual detail.

16 Supernature
Lyall Watson

Lyall Watson has a wide-ranging interest in natural and supernatural phenom-
ena of all kinds. He worked under Desmond Morris at the London Zoo and
pursued research in archaeology in the Middle East, in anthropology in Nigeria
and in marine biology in the Indian Ocean. His publications include *Omnivore:
our evolution in the eating game* (1971) and *The Romeo Error: a matter of life and
death* (1974).

A

1   In 1967 a Kiev film company produced a costly professional film
about a middle-aged Leningrad housewife. She is shown sitting at a
table in a physiology laboratory after being medically examined and
X-rayed to ensure that nothing is hidden on or in her body. She puts
out her hands, with the fingers spread, about six inches above a   5
compass in the center of the table and tenses her muscles. She stares
intently at the compass, lines etched deeply into her face showing the
strain of a body under acute tension. Minutes pass and sweat breaks
out on her brow as she continues the struggle, and then, slowly, the
compass needle quivers and moves to point in a new direction. She   10
starts to move her hands in a circular motion and the needle turns
with them, until it is rotating like the second hand on a watch. The
field produced by the body can, under certain conditions, it seems, be
stronger even than the field of earth itself.

2   There are many instances on record of matter apparently being   15
directly controlled in this way. Most deal with grandfather clocks
that 'stopped short, never to go again, when the old man died,' or
with pictures that fell from the wall at the precise moment of some
distant calamity. By their nature, events of this order are un-
repeatable and yield nothing to further analysis. They are lumped   20
together under the name of telekinesis – the ability to move things
from afar – and effectively ignored by all except hard-core
parapsychologists, but once in a while someone is discovered who
seems to be able to move things from afar on demand.

3   The most impressive of all early laboratory tests on this phenom-   25
enon was arranged in London by Harry Price, who made a name for
himself in the thirties as a highly skeptical investigator of ghosts. His

61

subject in this test was a young girl, and the task he set her was to depress a telegraph key that closed a circuit and lit a small red light bulb, without touching any of the apparatus. He made the test 30 difficult by blowing a mixture of soap and glycerine into a large bubble and placing this carefully over the whole apparatus. The bubble was then imprisoned under a glass cover, which was enclosed in a wire-net cage that stood in the center of a latticework fence of wood. Despite all these barriers, witnesses report that the girl was 35 able to make the light bulb flash on and off several times and that, at the conclusion of the test, the soap bubble was found to be intact. This is a neat demonstration and seems to have been honestly reported, but like most older experiments on the occult, it has loopholes which modern scientists pounce on and hold up to 40 ridicule. The report fails to say whether the key was seen to move, which could be important, because we now know that it is possible to induce current from a distance.

4   The whole pattern of investigation changed in 1934 when a lecturer in the psychology department at Duke University, in North 45 Carolina, was approached by a young gambler who claimed that he could control the fall of dice by willpower. The lecturer was J. B. Rhine, already involved in a long-term statistical study of telepathy, but what the gambler showed him right there on the office floor was enough to start him off on an entirely new track.   50

5   Rhine and his friends bought some ordinary plastic dice and began throwing them. They actively tried to will two dice to fall so that the total of their sides added up to more than seven. There are thirty-six possible combinations of two dice, and fifteen of these are greater than seven, so they expected to hit their target 2,810 times out 55 of 6,744 throws. They actually scored 3,110, which was so far from chance coincidence that it could occur only once in well over a billion times. Rhine concluded that it was possible that the mind could influence the fall of the dice, and so he set out to investigate what he called 'psychokinesis' – physical motion produced by the mind.   60

6   Tests of this kind had been made before, but what Rhine brought to investigation of the occult was a scientific method based on statistical analysis of large numbers of tests. The value of his system is shown clearly in this first test. Here the average rate of scoring should have been fifteen out of thirty-six, but it turned out to be 16.5. 65 Such a small deviation can easily be ignored in one test, but when it occurs over hundreds of tests it takes on an entirely different meaning, whose significance can be assessed only by sophisticated statistical analysis. This is not just mathematical juggling, but a method of defining what can reasonably be ascribed to coincidence 70 and what must be taking place for some other reason. In most

scientific research, a result is said to be significant if it would have occurred by chance alone no more than five out of a hundred times, which is odds of nineteen to one, but Rhine deliberately took extra precautions by ignoring anything that could have occurred by chance more than one out of a hundred times. 75

7   After twenty-five years of testing, Rhine concludes that 'the mind does have a force that can affect physical matter directly.' He feels that the weight of evidence in favor of psychokinesis (PK) is so great that 'merely to repeat PK tests with the single objective of finding 80 more evidence of the PK effect itself should be an unthinkable waste of time.'

·   ·   ·   ·   ·   ·

B

8 On a February morning in 1966 Cleve Backster made a discovery that changed his life and could have far-reaching effects on ours. Backster was at that time an interrogation specialist who left the 85 CIA to operate a New York school for training policemen in the techniques of using the polygraph, or 'lie detector'. This instrument normally measures the electrical resistance of the human skin, but on that morning he extended its possibilities. Immediately after watering an office plant, he wondered if it would be possible to measure the 90 rate at which water rose in the plant from the root to the leaf by recording the increase in leaf-moisture content on a polygraph tape. Backster placed the two psychogalvanic-reflex (PGR) electrodes on either side of a leaf of *Dracaena massangeana*, a potted rubber plant, and balanced the leaf into the circuitry before watering the plant 95 again. There was no marked reaction to this stimulus, so Backster decided to try what he calls 'the threat-to-well-being principle, a well-established method of triggering emotionality in humans'. In other words he decided to torture the plant. First of all he dipped one of its leaves into a cup of hot coffee, but there was no reaction, so he 100 decided to get a match and burn the leaf properly. 'At the instant of this decision, at thirteen minutes and fifty-five seconds of chart time, there was a dramatic change in the PGR tracing pattern in the form of an abrupt and prolonged upward sweep of the recording pen. I had not moved, or touched the plant, so the timing of the PGR pen 105 activity suggested to me that the tracing might have been triggered by the mere thought of the harm I intended to inflict on the plant.'

9   Backster went on to explore the possibility of such perception in the plant by bringing some live brine shrimp into his office and dropping them one by one into boiling water. Every time he killed a 110 shrimp, the polygraph recording needle attached to the plant jumped violently. To eliminate the possibility of his own emotions producing

this reaction, he completely automated the whole experiment so that an electronic randomiser chose odd moments to dump the shrimp into hot water when no human was in the laboratory at all. The plant *115* continued to respond in sympathy to the death of every shrimp and failed to register any change when the machine dropped already dead shrimp into the water.

10   Impressed by the plant's apparent sensitivity to stress, Backster collected specimens of other species and discovered that a philoden- *120* dron seemed to be particularly attached to him. He no longer handles this plant with anything but the greatest care, and whenever it is necessary to stimulate it in order to produce a reaction, his assistant, Bob Henson, 'plays the heavy'. Now the plant produces an agitated polygraph response every time Henson comes into the *125* room, and seems to 'relax' when Backster comes near or even speaks in an adjoining room. Enclosing the plant in a Faraday screen or a lead container has no effect, and it seems that the signals to which it responds do not fall within the normal electromagnetic spectrum. In more recent experiments Backster has found that fresh fruit and *130* vegetables, mold cultures, amoebae, paramecia, yeast, blood, and even scrapings from the roof of a man's mouth all show similar sensitivity to other life in distress.

11   This phenomenon, which Backster calls 'primary perception', has been substantiated by repetition of his work in other laboratories. It *135* raises awesome biological and moral questions; since thinking about it, I for one have had to give up mowing lawns altogether, but if it were to be taken to its logical limits we would end up, like the community in Samuel Butler's *Erewhon*, eating nothing but cabbages that have been certified to have died a natural death. The *140* answer to the moral problem lies in treating all life with respect, and killing, with real reluctance, only that which is necessary for survival – but the biological problems are not as easily resolved.

From *Supernature*

---

1   **a**   Suggest a title for each of these extracts, **A** and **B**.

    b   Bearing in mind the title *Supernature*, the book from which these extracts are taken, say:

       (i) what you think the overall theme of the book is
       (ii) how each extract contributes to this theme.

c Paragraphs 1–3 provide three examples of the author's topic:

  (i) the Leningrad housewife
  (ii) clocks and pictures
  (iii) the young girl.

What words or phrases in each paragraph suggest that the author accepts, rejects, or has reservations about the evidence given?

d Is Watson more or less impressed by Rhine's experiments *(paragraphs 4–7)* than by the preceding examples?

e What is his attitude to Backster's experiments (paragraphs 8–11)?

2 a (i) How would you define 'skeptical' – note the American spelling – *(line 27)*?
  (ii) According to your degree of scepticism in each case, arrange the five examples in **A** and **B** in order of precedence. Say why you are most/least sceptical about 1 and 5 in your list.

b (i) Give in your own words the main **hypothesis** (= a theory which needs further testing or research) suggested by each extract.
  (ii) Suggest hypotheses concerning *two* of the following:

  A a tenth planet in the solar system
  B the apparently increasing severity of British winters
  C wife-beating and early marriage
  D football hooliganism
  E the difference between the language of men and of women.

  (iii) Say which field of study each example belongs to.

c Without looking back at the extracts, can you now **define**:

  (i) telekinesis
  (ii) a parapsychologist
  (iii) psychokinesis?

d How many of these other **technical terms** (all mentioned in Watson's book *Supernature*) can you define:

astrology, autosuggestion, clairvoyance, ESP, exobiology, graphology, hallucination, horoscope, hypnosis, metempsychosis, palmistry, poltergeist, precognition, telepathy, zombie?

e State or deduce from the **context** the meaning of these:

(i) 'polygraph' *(line 92)* (ii) 'psycho-galvanic reflex electrodes' *(line 93)* (iii) 'electronic randomiser' *(line 114)* (iv) 'philodendron' *(lines 120–121)* (v) 'Faraday Screen' *(line 127)* (iv) 'electromagnetic spectrum' *(line 129)*.

3 Write a short piece on one of the following (words like 'phenomenon', 'demonstration', 'experiment', 'scientific', 'coincidence', 'research', 'substantiate' – all used in these extracts – might help you):

Mesmer, Uri Geller, séances, the planchette, Lourdes, exorcism.

17 Happiness
Malcolm Muggeridge

Malcolm Muggeridge's many years as a journalist took him to various parts of the world, including Moscow and Calcutta. He served in the 1939–45 war and was decorated with the Légion d'Honneur and the Croix de Guerre. In 1950 he become Deputy Editor of *The Daily Telegraph* and in 1953 the Editor of *Punch*. His many books include *The Thirties* (1940), *Jesus Rediscovered* (1969) and two parts of a three-volume autobiography, *The Chronicles of Wasted Time* (1972, 1973). He has been described as a 'non-aligned Christian'.

1 The sister-in-law of a friend of Dr Johnson was imprudent enough once to claim in his presence that she was happy. He pounced on her hard, remarking in a loud, emphatic voice that if she was indeed the contented being she professed herself to be, then her life gave the lie to every research of humanity; for she was happy without health,   *5* without beauty, without money and without understanding.

2   It was rough treatment, for which Johnson has been much criticised, though it should be remembered that he spoke as an eighteenth-century man, before our present preoccupation with happiness as an enduring condition of life became prevalent. *10* Actually, I think I see his point.

3   There is something quite ridiculous, and even indecent, in an individual claiming to be happy. Still more, a people or a nation making such a claim. The pursuit of happiness, included along with life and liberty in the American Declaration of Independence as an *15* inalienable right, is without any question the most fatuous which could possibly be undertaken. This lamentable phrase – the pursuit of happiness – is responsible for a good part of the ills and miseries of the modern world.

4   To pursue happiness, individually or collectively, as a conscious *20* aim is the surest way to miss it altogether; as is only too tragically evident in countries like Sweden and America where happiness has been most ardently pursued and where the material circumstances usually considered conducive to happiness have been most effect-ively constructed. The Gadarene swine were doubtless in pursuit of *25* happiness when they hurled themselves to destruction over the cliff. Today, the greater part of mankind, led by the technologically most

advanced, are similarly bent, and if they persist, will assuredly meet a similar fate. The pursuit of happiness, in any case, soon resolves itself into the pursuit of pleasure, something quite different. Pleasure is but *30* a mirage of happiness; a false vision of shade and refreshment seen across parched sand.

5   Where, then, does happiness lie? In forgetfulness, not indulgence, of the self. In escape from sensual appetites, not in their satisfaction. We live in a dark, self-enclosed prison which is all we see or know if *35* our glance is fixed ever downwards. To lift it upwards, becoming aware of the wide, luminous universe outside – this alone is happiness.

6   At its highest level such happiness is the ecstasy which mystics have inadequately described. At more humdrum levels it is human love; *40* the delights and beauties of our dear earth, its colours and shapes and sounds; the enchantment of understanding and laughing, and all other exercise of such faculties as we possess; the marvel of the meaning of everything, fitfully glimpsed, inadequately expounded, but ever-present.   *45*

7   Such is happiness – not compressible into a pill; not translatable into a sensation; lost to whomever would grasp it to himself alone, not to be gorged out of a trough, or torn out of another's body, or paid into a bank or driven along on another route, or fired in gun-salutes or discovered in the stratosphere. Existing, intangible, *50* in every true response to life, and absent in every false one. Pro-pounded through the centuries in every noteworthy word and thought and deed. Expressed in art and literature and music; in vast cathedrals and tiny melodies; in everything that is harmonious and in the unending heroism of imperfect men reaching *55* after perfection.

8   When Pastor Bonhoeffer was taken off by his Nazi guards to be executed, as I have read, his face was shining with happiness, to the point that even those poor clowns noted it. In that place of darkest evil, he was the happiest man – he the executed. 'For you it is an end,' *60* he told his executioners, 'but for me a beginning.' I find this an image of supreme happiness.

From *Woman's Hour: A Selection*

1   a   What did Dr Johnson mean when he said that the woman's life 'gave the lie to every research of humanity'? *(lines 4–5)*

b Health, beauty, money, understanding: which of these do you consider make the most and the least important contributions to happiness? Why?

c How would you distinguish between pleasure and happiness?

2 a (i) What is Malcolm Muggeridge's attitude to the pursuit of happiness?
  (ii) Quote six words or phrases from paragraphs 3 and 4 which help to convey this attitude.

b What does the author have in mind when he refers to 'the material circumstances usually considered conducive to happiness'? *(lines 23–24)*

c In paragraph 7 a number of ideas are **implicit**; e.g. 'not compressible into a pill' **implies**, in the **context**, that the sensations obtained by taking a drug are not of true happiness.

  (i) Give the **implication** of 'lost to whomever would grasp it to himself alone *(line 47)* and 'tiny melodies' *(line 54)*
  (ii) give the implication of four other such phrases in the paragraph, two concerning the absence and two the presence of happiness.

d By meeting unfamiliar words in various contexts, we bring them into our **receptive vocabulary** (words we recognise) and later into our **productive vocabulary** (words we use).

Place these words into the categories 'unfamiliar', 'receptive' or 'productive'. From the context guess the meaning of the unfamiliar ones and check your answer from the dictionary:

'imprudent' *(line 1)* 'emphatic' *(line 3)* 'preoccupation' *(line 9)* 'prevalent' *(line 10)* 'inalienable' *(line 16)* 'fatuous' *(line 16)* 'ardently' *(line 23)* 'conducive' *(line 24)* 'bent' *(line 28)* 'satisfaction' *(line 34)* 'mystics' *(line 39)* 'expounded' *(line 44)*.

3 'Dear Mr Muggeridge,

I've just been reading your short essay on happiness, which has made me think about my life and wonder about other people's, including your own. I'd like to ask you a few questions . . .'

Finish this letter.

18 Seconds Out
Michael Osborne

Michael Osborne sent this note on his career: Born at Scunthorpe, Lincolnshire, in 1949. Cannot remember a time when he was not literate, and won a bar of chocolate for reading the first leader in the *Manchester Guardian* at the age of three. Was idle and truculent at grammar school. Drifted into journalism *faute de mieux* at eighteen, working first in Norwich, then Coventry, Leeds and Manchester before ending up in Fleet Street. Publications: none, apart from headlines such as BREAD MAN USES HIS LOAF AND BERSERK VAMPIRE SEIZED IN COFFIN. Interests: reading jewelled and magnificent prose, smoking and metaphysics.

———————

1   When God made time, as people used to say, He made plenty of it. Now everyone is wearing multi-function digital chronometers fitted with stopwatch, alarm, day, date, leap-year adjustment, calculator, personal biorhythm computer, and the exact time anywhere from Valparaiso to Vienna at the pop of a knob. All correct to the nearest   5
tenth of a second, and continuing so for the next aeon before changing the battery.

2   What, I wonder, do we do with these tenths of seconds realised so ingeniously? I have a feeling that, although God made plenty of time, we've put it down somewhere and forgotten where the devil it   10
is.

3   Not so many millennia ago you'd ask what the time was and the chap would squint at the sun, spit on the ground, roll the thought round in his head and say 'Tuesday'. Say you had an appointment for Friday: you'd turn up just as the sun was climbing over the local   15
megalith, lean incuriously on a gate and chew a field of straws while waiting. Perhaps the man would turn up – perhaps he might not come till Saturday – but it wouldn't matter much because eternity was not humming away, second by second, on your wrist while you fretted about your business lunch with some Druids.   20

4   Then the slide began. Blame the Romans – but not too much. The day was cracked up into hours, but for them nine o'clock, say, was not the same as nine o'clock for us. To Julius Caesar, nine was any time between half past eight and half past nine. To us it is a mere smut on the nose of eternity. That's why Caesar had time to conquer   25

all three parts of Gaul. That's why he had to beware the whole Ides of
March, not 11.37 am. And twenty seconds.
5   But that wasn't the end of it. Some genius got the notion of
hoisting half a ton of ironmongery and oak beams up a church
tower, and thus invented the clock. I'd tell you his name, but I don't
have time to look it up. This man's clocks, of course, only had an
hour hand. Doubtless he was bright enough to have stuck on a
minute hand too if there'd been any call for it, but there wasn't; you
can't plough a field or debauch a nunnery in one sixtieth of an hour.
So he made just one hand, but the rot had set in.
6   Minutes, for all practical purposes, came later, when we'd already
mislaid time somewhere and were beginning to wonder where it was.
But hours and minutes together would be good enough for the next
few centuries, except for such arcane purposes as sailing off round
the world to civilise black folks; good enough, really, until seventy
or eighty years ago. There are several records about of
Mr Gladstone speaking (strange how he still commands a
Mr; Disraeli is Dizzied everywhere like some chat-show host or
champion golfer, but no-one calls Gladstone Gladdie). Sonorous,
rolling, slow and particular as evolution, Mr Gladstone would have
been in the early afternoon before he'd finished saying good
morning. There was still lots of time about in Mr Gladstone's day –
but the rot was creeping deeper.
7   Then – but not finally, for there's another age to run yet – came
the second. I don't know what *caused* the second. Maybe it was the
Great War, when gunnery officers and generals bristled around
synchronising watches so everyone could be blown up at the same
instant, which made for elegant schedules. Doubtless there were
seconds before the war, but I suspect people didn't have much use for
them. Like aeroplanes, they must have been an interesting
peculiarity, but unlikely to catch on.
8   And now, heaven help us all, we know the time to the nearest tenth
of a second. There it is, winking on my wrist. Is it winking on yours?
Put it another way: each day we can plan to dispose of our valuable
time to one part in 864,000. (It must take hours to plan so closely.)
We can say with all the enthusiasm of the technologically *nouveau
riche*, 'Meet me at four thirty-two and eleven point seven seconds
under the quartz crystal digital public chronometer at Waterloo' –
but we've wasted 5.7 seconds saying it.
9   There must be some purpose to this infinite division of eternity. I
suppose it gives us the illusion that, having more bits of time at our
disposal, time as a whole has grown bigger and we can accomplish
more in it. But infinity, however divided, is still infinity. What we do
accomplish – look around you tomorrow as you travel to work – is

stomach ulcer, nagging harassment, neurosis, and the general 70
suspicion that there's a monkey sitting on your back and that you
can't shake him off.

10   It is pleasing to imagine some megalomaniac potentate taking a
whim to banish the second hand from his dominions. He might as
well banish the minute hand too, and all his subjects would run their 75
lives to the nearest hour. Practice makes perfect in patience, as in
other things, and they'd all get so used to hanging around watching
the mountains erode that patience would flourish like the National
Debt, and Roche would have to scrape a living out of cough drops.

11   I hope it is no condemning confession of inadequacy to admit I 80
never understood Einstein. The space-time continuum, as applied to
newspapers, is quite clear: if you have time to write a story they've no
space to print it, and if they have the space you don't have the time.
But that's as far as I get. I do understand Pope, though, when he
observed, 'Man never *is* but always *to be* blest'. If the present wasn't 85
long enough for the leisurely eighteenth century, what on earth can
we do in a tenth of a second?

From *The Observer* magazine, 23 September, 1979

═══════════

1 a What is time?

   b What has Michael Osborne to say about

      (i) time in the past
      (ii) time at present?

   c Attempt to prove or disprove Osborne's claim that 'infinity,
      however divided, is still infinity.' *(line 68)*

   d Say if and why you would support or not support the
      'megalomaniac potentate' *(line 73)* in banishing second and
      minute hands from his dominion.

   e If Osborne's general **thesis** is correct, what may happen to time in
      the future?

2 a Though the theme of the essay is serious, the **tone** is humorous.
      Find examples of these points which contribute to the humour:

(i) **informal** expressions (ii) **puns** (iii) **irony** (iv) **incongruity** (v) **exaggeration** or **hyperbole**.

b What other points seem to you interesting in the tone or style of the piece?

c What do you have to know to appreciate the **allusions** to:

'biorhythm' *(line 4)* 'megalith' *(line 16)* 'Julius Caesar' *(line 23)* 'the *nouveau riche*' *(lines 61–62)* 'the National Debt' *(lines 78–79)* 'Roche' *(line 79)* 'Einstein' *(line 81)*?

3 a What points would you raise in an argument against Osborne's ideas?

b What would happen to time if man became extinct?

c Write a paragraph on one of these:

(i) 'Man never *is*, but always *to be* blest.'
(ii) Time Machines.
(iii) 'Time must have a stop.'

19 The Function of the Dream
J. A. Hadfield

J. A. Hadfield studied arts and theology at Oxford and medicine at Edinburgh. Most of his career, in both peace and war, was devoted to psychology and neurology. He was a founder member of the Tavistock Clinic. His books include *Psychology and Mental Health* (1950), *Mental Health and the Psychoneuroses* (1952) and *Childhood and Adolescence* (1952).

1 According to what we shall call the Biological Theory of dreams, the function of dreams is that by means of reproducing the unsolved experience of life, they work towards a solution of these problems . . . .

2   Let us take the simplest kind of objective dream. A man who when   *5* climbing a cliff had had a slight slip, but had come to no harm, that night dreamt he was cliff-climbing, slipped, and had a terrifying fall as he hurtled to the ground, and woke up with a start. The next night he had the same dream, but in falling he tried to clutch a passing stump of a tree or jutting rock, and again woke with a start. On   *10* successive nights he dreamt the same thing, but ultimately he did catch the jutting rock and so saved himself. Now the effect of this series of dreams is that if he is subjected to such an experience again, which he is liable to have as a cliff-climber, he is better able to cope with the situation, for he has now been through the experience not   *15* once but a dozen times. Such repetitive dreams are very common to airmen who have crashed, to soldiers and civilians who have been blown up or buried, and who sometimes for months or years continue to have war dreams, and to most of us if we have even slight car accidents which might have had serious consequences.   *20*

3   These dreams clearly indicate the biological function of dreams. In the first place, *dreams stand in the place of experience*. Thus by making us relive the experiences and difficulties of the day in imagination they relieve us of the necessity of going through the actual experiences by trial and error and thus save us from many a   *25* disaster.

4   Secondly, by making us relive these experiences, often in an exaggerated form, they warn us of the possible consequences of our actions, and may indeed prevent us cliff-climbing by producing a

phobia for cliffs, or deter us from ever taking the risk again by *30* producing a 'nervous breakdown'.

5   Thirdly, by reliving these experiences dreams work towards a solution of the problems. That is the significance of the repetitive nature of the dream: the unsolved problem is perpetually thrust into consciousness until we attend to it and solve it.   *35*

6   Thus if a novice is sailing unwarily, has a sudden gybe and nearly capsizes, he may dream first of actually capsizing, and perhaps even drowning, for the first dream of such an event is usually an exaggeration, and he wakes up in a start. This exaggeration of the consequences of his action serves to warn him of its dangers even *40* more than the experience itself. But as he continues to dream of the incident the next night and the next, he finds himself coping with the situation by righting the craft before it capsizes, either by turning into the wind or letting out the sheet gradually, and so he becomes more skilled in dealing with this problem the next time he meets it. *45*

7   To take a more subjective problem: a man has trouble with his boss in business and he has to submit. This rankles in his mind, yet he cannot do otherwise than give in for fear of losing his job. But he has a dream in which he stands up to his boss, and to his surprise his boss respects him the more. This dream makes him realise that it is *50* because he cringes that his boss despises him and that by having more confidence in himself he will win the respect of others. He previously felt he ought to do something about it, but did not. The dream, by making him actually do so, encouraged him in fact to take up that attitude with gratifying results. The dream stands in the place *55* of experience and helps towards a solution of his problem.

8   In the pursuance of this aim and purpose, dreams have certain characteristics which we may study.

9   In the first place, dreams are essentially reproductive: this is the most popular and, so far, correct view of dreams. They may be direct *60* and literal reproductions of events of the day, or they may be reiterations of events in our remote past such as terrifying experiences of infancy which often appear as nightmares and are reproduced as phobias. Or they may be reproductions not so much of events but of problems and worries which in the dream may be *65* expressed in symbolic form.

10   If, however, we examine these experiences we shall find that they are rarely *exact* reproductions of what occurred during the day, nor are they by any means the most important events of the day: indeed they are often of the most trifling nature. Nor are they necessarily the *70* events with the greatest emotional tone. But if we study them more closely we shall always find that they are experiences which are in some way connected with an unsolved problem or worry. The

experiences of our childhood which we dream about are always those which we were unable to cope with at that time – for those fears and situations with which we were able to deal adequately leave no unsolved problem behind to worry us. These terrifying experiences of childhood persist and reproduce themselves throughout childhood until they may be solved by the greater confidence of adolescence, when they tend to pass away; or they may persist through life. 75

80

From *Dreams and Nightmares*

========

1 a Dreams have always fascinated mankind. Suggest three reasons, not given in the extract, for this fascination.

b (i) In one sentence summarise the three aspects the writer gives of the biological function of dreams in lines 21–35.
(ii) What, in your view, is a biologically successful species? How could the writer's ideas on dreams be related to this idea?

c (i) Show how the writer divides the three dreams mentioned into three **categories**.
(ii) Recount or invent a dream suitable for each category and say how a 'problem' might be solved in each case.

2 a (i) From the **context** guess the meaning of these **technical terms**:
'phobia' *(lines 30 and 64)* – from psychology; 'gybe' *(line 36)* and 'sheet' *(line 44)* – from sailing.
(ii) State or find out the meaning of:
agoraphobia, anglophobia, claustrophobia, hydrophobia, xenophobia.

b 'Dreams are essentially reproductive'. The writer makes this **generalisation** which he then **qualifies** by five further points in lines 61–71. Say what these five points are.

c (i) Is the meaning of **'symbolic'** *(line 66)*, **implicit** or **explicit** in the extract?
(ii) Later in the book the writer gives this example of dream symbolism: 'A patient sees herself in a hard stiff dress in

which she can scarcely move; after that she sees herself in hospital. Then she is in the Lake District climbing a mountain which she finds difficult; and her father is dead.'

The writer explains that the patient's dream 'is trying to say pictorially what the logical mind would express in words by saying that her life has hitherto been too restricted, too cramped and hidebound . . . she has lived in a strait-jacket.'

How would you interpret the other symbolic elements in the dream?

3 a In what way might (i) a day-dream (ii) an animal's dream be different from those described by the writer?

 b If there were a dream-prevention pill, would you take it?

 c Relate a dream which a person famous in history might have dreamt at a critical point in his/her life.

20 Their Time is Nearly Run Out
Ruth Harrison

Ruth Harrison's book deals with modern animal husbandry, which, as Rachel Carson says in her Foreword, 'has been swept by a passion for "intensivism". On this tide everything that resembles the methods of an earlier day has been carried away.' Ruth Harrison ends her detailed survey by looking at the economic, moral and legal aspects of what she calls 'production line methods applied to the rearing of animals.'

=====

1 We made our way down to the innocuous-looking factory-like building. On the outside of the vast shed with its great sliding doors hundreds of crates were stacked high against the wall, just as they had been unloaded from the lorries.

2　White overalls and wellington boots were sent for to protect us 　5 from the blood in the slaughter room and then we went into the shed. More crates were stacked up the inside wall, twelve birds to the crate, with a grandstand view of all that went on: the noise and bustle, the music-while-you-work, the harsh light, the throb and clatter of machinery. They had come, these ten-week-old birds, from their 　10 dimmed out, hushed and cossetted environment, protected from any unusual noise or disturbance. They had been bundled into crates and on to lorries and for the first time had seen God's own sun above their heads. For the first time and the last time. They had come to the end of their journey.　15

3　Not that they could have been in an ideal frame of mind to savour the full benison of their brief period in the light. As in all slaughtering, the birds are advisedly starved for twelve to sixteen hours before they reach the packing station and they are apt to spend the best part of a day in their crates after they reach it, before their 　20 turn comes. During this time they get neither food nor drink, because any undigested food is waste and can impair the keeping quality of the carcase in the deep freeze. In this business a half ounce of food per bird is big money, it could mean the difference between a profit and a loss.　25

4　Their time is nearly run out. Taken out of their crates they are suspended by their legs on a moving belt, gently because they mustn't be frightened or they would not defeather so well! The time taken to reach the slaughterman varies between one and five minutes according to the layout and speed of the conveyor belt. As they move along their beaks open and shut, mutely, in what has all the appearance of fear, but I was told that chickens are dim creatures and have not the slightest idea of what is happening to them. When they reared up and flapped their wings a gentle pulling down on their necks assured quiet hanging and on they went.

5   I noticed that there was a time when for about half a minute they passed within a few feet of the conveyor belt moving in the opposite direction bearing the other chickens, still shackled, but already defeathered, and that it was at this time that they showed most symptoms of fear. Was I deceiving myself? Was it a coincidence? On a latter occasion I asked the naturalist Konrad Lorenz whether he thought they would realise what was happening and he replied: 'According to my experience, chickens do not "understand" the situation when their fellows are being slaughtered or lying dead, it certainly would not increase their suffering. Conversely, I am convinced that cattle suffer the torments of extreme terror when entering the slaughterhouse because they do smell the blood of their own species.' A distinguished poultryman, on the other hand, seems to differ. Murray Hale writing in *Poultry World* (5 October 1961) said:

6   ' . . . The awareness of danger is the only thing that enables a species to survive in the wild, and no amount of domestication can eradicate these deep-seated instincts. Genetically they are not only dominant, they are paramount.'

and Mr Fry of Reading wrote to *Poultry World* (22 June 1961):

7   ' . . . All the consumer wants is a clean, well-fleshed wholesome looking bird. Where this is not achieved I think the packing station may be more to blame than the grower.

8   In a good many instances birds are piled in crates on the floor in full view of their colleagues being slaughtered and there is no doubt but that they know what is in store for them. This frightens them and a scared tensed-up bird does not pluck well, in my opinion, because the grip on its feathers is increased.'

9   Some packing stations have stunners to use before the birds have their throats cut, some do not. Some have stunners but do not use them. The one I visited was one of these latter. 'They do not bleed properly,' said the manager, 'it is much quicker this way, and kinder too.' I watched the birds having their throats cut and disappear, flapping wildly, into the bleeding tunnel, to reappear a minute later still flapping wildly, to go into the scalding tank. 'They are dead

before they go into that,' said the manager reassuringly. When the birds came through the scalding tank they were limp and dead. They then went through a defeathering machine and at this point were conveyed past the live birds and through a gap in the wall into the evisceration room. In the evisceration room the conveyor belt moved *75* slowly over a bench running the length of the hall, with a gulley underneath for waste. Along this bench stood dozens of white-coated young girls and men and as the conveyor belt moved they each did their 'piece work'. One weighed the bird, the next cut off its feet and resuspended it on the belt this time by its head, the next slit it *80* open and so on. When it was thoroughly clean, inside and out, it went through a chilling machine and the conveyor belt then passed into a third room where final shaping and packaging into polythene bags went on. Here any bruised or battered birds were removed and cut into 'chicken pieces', the disfigured parts being removed first. *85* The polythene packs are piled into wire trolleys which are duly wheeled into the deep freeze rooms for storage until a sale is made. At this time the frozen packs are put into gay cardboard boxes showing some happy picture to attract the house-wife's attention in the supermarket or store. *90*

10 There was a general air of contentment amongst the workers: the girls hummed and the men chatted. Even in the slaughter room people walked casually around, pushing the birds to one side, like curtains, if they were in the way, and then if the birds seemed disturbed, pulling their necks to quieten them again. The whole *95* process, from crate to deep freeze takes between eighteen minutes and upwards of an hour depending on the rate of the line.

11 'Do you eat broiler chickens?' we asked the manager. Back came the prompt reply, 'Good lord, no!'

From *Animal Machines*

1 **a** What is the writer's purpose in this passage?

  b Say if and why you think she is successful.

2 Cicero said: '**Irony** is the saying of one thing and meaning another.'

  Say which of the following items from the passage are, in your view, ironic, and in what way:

a 'innocuous-looking' *(line 1)*
b 'a grandstand view of all that went on' *(line 8)*
c 'hushed and cossetted environment' *(line 11)*
d 'not that they could have been in an ideal frame of mind to savour the full benison of their brief period in the light' *(lines 16–17)*
e 'half an ounce of food per bird is big money' *(lines 23–24)*
f 'a gentle pulling down on their necks assured quiet hanging' *(lines 34–35)*
g 'There was a general air of contentment' *(line 91)*

3 **a** 'They do not bleed properly, it is much quicker this way, and kinder too.' *(lines 66–68)*

Comment on the arguments in this statement, taking them separately and together.

b Discuss the following:

'We believe that while it is not legitimate to use one human being, without his consent, as a means to another's end, it is, within certain limits, legitimate to use animals for human ends. This assumption lies behind our use of animals and their products as food, our exclusion of animals from their natural environment for the benefit of humans . . . If there were not some such general assumption, all infliction of pain on animals (except for their own good) would be cruelty.'

From a Home Office Report, quoted in *The Times*, 29 January, 1980

21 Fox-hunting Debate
(various authors)

The following letters were all printed in *The Scotsman* newspaper during September and October 1980.

=======

A   20 August, 1980

1 Sir, – If Lothian Region see fit to ban fox hunting on their land I
suggest that they also ban the use of eggs and chicken meat in their
school dinners.

2 A hunted fox has a very fair chance of escape under one of nature's 5
strongest laws, the survival of the fittest.

3 The battery hen has no chance whatsoever of leading a normal life.

4 Misplaced and ignorant sentimentality is a characteristic of anti-
hunting cranks, but is better avoided by a responsible public body
such as a regional council.   10

Shirley Page

B   26 August, 1980

5 Sir, – As an anti-cruelty to all animals crank, I was most interested to
read Shirley Page's letter comparing fox-hunting favourably with
the battery hen industry.   15

6 It was a revelation to me that fox-hunters hunted down the animal
for food. This being so, may I suggest that having a terrified animal
torn to pieces alive by a large number of dogs is a very inefficient
method of getting it into the pot and on to the table? (Is there,
incidentally, a book of fox recipes?) Imagine the inconvenience of 20
having to go round collecting a paw and an ear here, a lung and some
intestines there, or having to deal with a disembowelled fox that isn't
quite dead.

7 May I suggest shooting the creature, thereby saving the money on
horses (with trappings), expensive blood-coloured outfits, whips, a 25
large number of dogs and cudgels to beat up any passing ignorant,

sentimental crank? I am fairly certain that most foxes are not masochists and would prefer this method.

8   Shooting would have the added advantage that fox-lovers (in the culinary sense) could have proper roast fox (with Yorkshire 30 pudding?) and would not be limited, as at present, to casseroles or to frying small pieces of fox in breadcrumbs.

9   I am sure Ms Page is particular about the company she keeps but if she *does* happen to know someone who enjoys running down a terrified animal and watch it being torn to pieces by dogs not even for 35 food but for *fun*, then I confess to having an unhealthy interest in hearing exactly what feelings are thereby aroused in such people – feelings they presumably need and enjoy.

10   Would Ms Page care to describe these feelings and put a name to someone who needs to indulge in them? 'Crank', I fear, is too 40 innocent an expression for such a one. I can think of one or two words myself if her English does not run to it. The activity has been described as the dumb pursued by the unspeakable, but I think we might manage to be more specific in a post-Freudian age.

Mary P. Scholan 45

C   31 August, 1980

11   Sir, – Mary Scholan's letter (August 26) shows the typical ignorance of a town-dweller to nature: if she is worrying about the feelings of a hunted fox, what about those of the nine of our lambs that we found one morning with their stomachs torn out by a vixen to take to her 50 cubs?

12   We shot her, but had we not been able to do so, we would have used poison or traps, both nasty, but necessary, to protect our livestock.

13   If asked, a fox would (in my opinion) infinitely prefer to be hunted, 55 where he has a sporting chance of escape.

14   Why does she not concentrate on the great cruelty in the big markets, where I have handled bullocks (mostly from Ireland) whose hindquarters were beaten almost to a jelly. Onlookers, in most but not all cases, did nothing to stop the beating. Or what about sending 60 frequently underwatered, or unwatered, animals on long journeys, under conditions where they cannot turn round, much less lie down?

15   These cruelties mostly take place in the big town markets.

16   It is odd that these town-dwellers concentratate on a minor cruelty in the countryside, and one which to me seems relatively unimportant, 65 and is almost always brought up by class-conscious or envious

cranks, who know nothing of nature's workings or of the real countryside.

17   I think I can safely add that the majority of hunt followers enjoy the run rather than the kill. Mary Scholan should concentrate on *70* methods of calf rearing for veal or, as I said, market and transport of animals, before she begins to worry about the feelings of the notoriously cruel and destructive fox.

Joyce Rutherford

D   2 September, 1980 *75*

18 Sir, – I doubt if it is possible to make a sensible reply to the curious reasoning of Mary P. Scholan with regard to the keeping of hens in batteries and the hunting of foxes but since she has clearly missed my point I suppose I had better try.

19   She suggests that foxes should be controlled by shooting. This is *80* extremely difficult to do with any degree of certainty and is likely to result in maimed or injured foxes dying a slow and painful death.

20   She seems to be worried that people who hunt might enjoy the killing part. Actually the enjoyment comes from watching the skill of hounds hunting and in the excitement of riding hard to keep up with *85* them when they get a good scent.

21   She makes no effort to defend the cruelty, which we all accept, which must be involved in the keeping of battery hens, and how does she know that the people who work in this industry do not enjoy what they are doing – maybe they even enjoy killing the hens? *90*

Shirley E. Page

E   4 September, 1980

22 Sir, – Joyce Rutherford's letter today is a copybook example of hunting lobby rhetoric. Those of us who regard this sport as an obscene charade, and have the temerity to say so in public, are *95* sweepingly dismissed as 'cranks' and 'town-dwellers'. Why, she asks, do we not concentrate on vivisection, factory farming, etc?

23   I have lived in both town and country, and have been actively involved in opposing fox-hunting. This has included a brush with the Linlithgow Hunt, whose response to opposition has been well-*100* documented recently. In my experience, those who make a stand against blood sports are also very involved in fighting cruel

laboratory treatment of animals, veal farming, and the rest of the degrading catalogue of cruelty going on all around us – in town and country. It is a very muddled morality which justifies something on *105* the grounds that worse things happen. Does the existence of rape make obscene phone calls acceptable?

24   The fact is that opponents of hunting are well aware of the damage foxes can inflict on farm stock, and sympathise with the farmers affected. However, shooting and poisons are infinitely more humane *110* and efficient methods of dealing with the problem. Joyce Rutherford obviously knows this, since she uses them herself.

25   As to the joys of the chase, and the need for horsepersons to exercise themselves and their steeds, surely this can be achieved by laying a trail for the hounds across country. The only thing lacking *115* from this method (known as 'drag hunting') is the final evisceration of the prey. If the hunting lobby think drag hunting unacceptable, we must conclude that the chase isn't the thing after all.

26   Joyce Rutherford's justifiable concern for animal welfare is obviously sincere. She does herself a disfavour to assume that such *120* concern is confined to rural dwellers, or is present at all the ranks of hunting adherents.

Keith Leadbetter

F   4 September, 1980

27 Sir, – Joyce Rutherford's letter today on fox-hunting illustrates, *125* with painful clarity, the poverty of argument to which its defenders are reduced and the confused mental processes which appear to be characteristic of the fraternity – a fact reinforced by my private correspondence! To be fair, neither Joyce Rutherford nor anyone else can defend an indefensible activity and I will merely add a few *130* points which may help her disentangle her ideas.

28   I have been privately taken to task, by the way, for calling the hounds 'dogs'. The point makes no difference to the argument, nor presumably, to the fox, unless, of course, there is a future switch to long-haired chihuahuas!   *135*

29   Joyce Rutherford makes no pretence that fox-hunting is anything but cruel, although I find her phrase 'minor cruelty' a chilling one. The fact that there are many other forms of cruelty to animals does not, of course, justify fox-hunting. I made it perfectly clear that I am opposed to all forms of cruelty to animals on land, in the sea, and in *140* the air. I did not initiate the correspondence on fox-hunting. That was done by Shirley Page.

30   A great point is made by fox-hunters about how 'cruel' the fox is

and how it 'deserves' its fate. Even we ignorant townies know, in an age of television, what some animals do to others. Animals will be *145* animals. Lions, sharks and female tarantulas, to name but a few, can behave horrendously, but they are never 'cruel'. As some doomed sailor tried, in vain, to tell Captain Ahab about Moby Dick, moral standards do not apply to brute beasts following their nature. Moral standards, however, do apply to humans, and fox-hunters are not *150* justified in behaving like foxes.

31   In my last letter, I raised the question of the debasing effect of the hunt on the hunters. Joyce Rutherford skates over the issue. 'The majority of hunt followers enjoy the run rather than the kill,' she says? Is this an admission that there is a minority of sadists? If the *155* majority enjoy merely the 'run', why don't they go for a ride on horseback? Why do they need an accompanying pack of hounds running down a terrified fox?

32   As for her remark that those of us who find fox-hunting disgusting are 'class-conscious or envious cranks', I find it difficult to dig out the *160* point of this apart from its being a childish attempt to be offensive. Would she care to elaborate? It is certainly true that fox-hunting has long been associated with titled and land-owning groups.

33   It is equally true that I do not belong to these groups. (How did she know?) I do not, however, think in stereotypes. I am prepared to *165* believe that there are many members of these groups who find fox-hunting as obscene as I do. On the other hand, I cannot accept that because an activity may be pursued by a lord, it is therefore morally acceptable. Such a view would be naive. De Sade, after all, was a marquis.   *170*

34   It seems to me that, apart from reducing considerably the suffering of the fox, the disappearance of the hunt would be one less outlet for the basest instincts in Man. Shoot the brutes, I say! I mean the foxes, of course!

Mary P. Scholan *175*

G   4 September, 1980

35 Sir, – Granted that some foxes must be killed, is it really necessary to dress up in funny clothes and make a sport out of it?

John L. Broom

H   25 September, 1980 *180*

36 Sir, – I have read with interest the fox-hunting debate in your columns over the last few weeks. Whilst the anti-hunting faction

have often displayed an incredible lack of understanding of the interaction of field sports and wild life in the countryside by their presentation of innaccurate 'facts', the pro-hunters have tried to *185* defend their stance by introducing issues like factory farming which have no direct bearing on the matter.

37   I wonder how many of the anti-hunt correspondents or indeed what proportion of the much publicised MORI poll interviewees have actually taken the trouble to spend some time following a hunt *190* to find out what really happens and why – not many I think. I certainly would not care to voice an opinion on any activity which I had not investigated firsthand with an open mind.

38   What is indisputable, however, is that the fox is a very successful, versatile and adaptable animal maintaining a healthy population, *195* ably assisted in the past by man who has eradicated its only serious ground predator, the wolf, and greatly reduced the range of its main avian predator, the golden eagle. In addition man has provided the fox with excellent cover in the form of ever-expanding forestry.

39   Furthermore, it is a fact that foxes *do* kill lambs (though *200* overstated on occasion), and game, and they are vectors of the killer disease, rabies, which is steadily marching towards this country. It seems reasonable, therefore, that man should keep the population at an acceptable level in the same way as he does with many other wild animals.   *205*

40   Foxes can be shot. The traditional way of doing this in lowland areas is by 'end of season' fox drives with shotguns in the spring, after the end of the game shooting season and before lambing and nesting time. Foxes are, however, *shot at* on sight by many people, particularly in non-hunting areas.   *210*

41   I emphasise *shot at* because I have lost count of the number of times I have seen shot-peppered foxes skulking off into cover or the number of times I have heard 'He's well hit, he won't go far.' The result in most cases is a lingering death from gangrene, lead poisoning or starvation. Snaring too is a traditional method, often, *215* though not always, used efficiently and humanely by gamekeepers. With fox pelts fetching up to £30 each in the London fur markets last winter, however, the amateur trappers were out in force with their irresponsibly set lines of self-locking snares, usually checked only at weekends. These characters have undoubtedly caused untold suffer- *220* ing to thousands of foxes, not to mention badgers and roe-deer.

42   Poisoning is illegal, though to listen to some of the anti-hunt brigade you may think otherwise – but it is nevertheless used. It is totally unselective, often causes secondary poisoning, and depending on the level of the intake and type of poison can result in a horrible *225* death.

43   All these methods kill foxes but I would submit that none is humane or guarantees a quick death. When a fox is hunted with hounds I would suggest that this can be likened to the reintroduction of a predator/prey relationship and that terror or fear probably only overtakes the animal's instincts for self-preservation at the last 230 moment when the hounds close in and the fox realises that the end is inevitable. Can any of the anti-hunt supporters provide substantial scientific evidence to the contrary? I further suggest that when condemning hunting many people tend to imagine themselves in the fox's position which is not a true analogy.   235

44   The 'sport' aspect of hunting seems to upset many people. The huntsman is a professional, who with his assistants and hounds is there to catch foxes. The followers are merely spectators who enjoy watching hounds work and riding or walking over countryside to which they would not normally have access. Although I have never 240 followed hounds on horseback it appears to me that the riders are rarely up with hounds at the kill.

45   Many opponents find the breaking up of the fox by hounds offensive. At this point the fox is dead, and like gazelle or zebra being torn apart by lions (a common sequence shown on television wildlife 245 programmes nowadays) is not likely to be particularly worried.

46   As an ecologist who has studied many field sports and is interested in the long term welfare of all wildlife in Britain, including foxes, I must concur with the views of (*the writer here refers to a letter not included in this sequence*) and will continue to support hunting as a 250 humane method of fox-destruction.

47   What I do find most objectionable is the way in which some of the anti-lobby are seeking to drag wild life into the political arena, supposedly in the name of animal welfare. In this connection it is significant that the Labour Party manifesto states that that party, if 255 returned to government, will introduce legislation to ban fox-hunting, beagling, horse-coursing and stag-hunting.

48   What is more significant, however, is that the two major field-sports, fishing and shooting, have been excluded from the list, not because they are more acceptable to the genuine moral objector but 260 because of the voting implication of trying to ban them.

Andrew J. Macfarlane

1 Choose *six* of the of the arguments given in the letters, three on each side of the debate, and say which one or more of the following categories you would put each into:

Relevant   Irrelevant   True   Untrue   Strong   Weak

2 What are the pros and cons of writing to the press as compared with any *two* other ways of expressing a viewpoint?

3 Write a letter to the press on one of these topics:

(i) Slimming (ii) The Older Generation (iii) The Younger Generation (iv) Nuclear Weapons (v) Corporal Punishment (vi) Any topic you feel strongly about.

22 Courting Customs
E. S. Turner

Ernest Sackville Turner is the author of a number of books which explore the byways of social history. His first, in 1948, was *Boys Will Be Boys*, a survey of popular boys' papers. Other titles include *The Shocking History of Advertising*, *A History of Courting*, *Amazing Grace* (the great days of dukes) and, in 1980, *Dear Old Blighty*, which describes events on the home front in 1914–18.

He has been a contributor to *Punch* since 1935 and is a member of the *Punch* Table. He also writes for the *Listener* and the *Times Literary Supplement*.

Born in Liverpool in 1909, E. S. Turner was educated in Shrewsbury and Newcastle-under-Lyme. He worked on newspapers in Glasgow in the 1930s, served in the Royal Artillery in the war, and from 1946–57, edited the magazine *Soldier* for the War Office. His chief diversion is travel. He met his first wife (who died in 1968) in New York and his second wife in Samarkand. His home is at Richmond-on-Thames.

A THE HEYDAY OF THE CHAPERON

1 Now was the heyday of the chaperon, that much-misunderstood functionary. Curiously, English etiquette books had little to say about her, whereas American writers on manners said a great deal. The chaperon might be the girl's mother, aunt or sister, or she might be a paid companion (like Dickens' Mrs General) drawn from a   5 good middle-class background; an officer's widow, perhaps. Her duty was to preside in the parlour when a potential suitor called, to accompany her young charge to balls, parties, dinners, routs, races and especially theatres. At all times she had to study the characters and manners of the young men who hovered round her protégée, to   10 try to divine their intentions and to check on their backgrounds (and fortunes). It could be a full-time job.

2   For a young girl, not too confident in herself, there were positive advantages in being chaperoned. She had her path smoothed for her by the older woman, who introduced her to likely young men and set   15 the stage, if need be, for a proposal. It will be remembered how Becky Sharp, in the gardens of Vauxhall, tried vainly to bring her East India Collector to say the requisite words:

3   'All she wanted was the proposal, and ah! how Rebecca now felt

the want of a mother! – a dear, tender mother, who would have 20
managed the business in ten minutes, and, in the course of a little
delicate, confidential conversation, would have extracted the interesting avowal from the bashful lips of the young man!'*

4 At a ball, if any young man proved over-attentive, a girl could
shake him off by making the excuse that she must return to her 25
chaperon; there was no reason why she should have to put up with
undesirable company. Equally the presence of a chaperon was a
blessing to a young man who found his partner dull. Instead of
having her on his hands all evening he was at perfect liberty to walk
her once round the floor after the dance and then hand her back to 30
her chaperon, pleading another engagement. If the two clearly
relished each other's company, the chaperon – so long as she
approved of the young man – would give them ample opportunities
to consent.

5 There were, of course, tyrannous chaperons, who usurped the 35
right to open their protégées' letters; conscienceless chaperons, who
did not mind what their girls did and spent their time gossiping at the
buffet; snobbish chaperons, who saw to it that their girls did not
waste too much time on curates and subalterns; flirtatious
chaperons, who set their charges a bad example; and tipsy 40
chaperons, who set a worse one. But most of them were sensible
women, neither duennas nor dupes, whose presence kept the
manners of the young generation at a higher level than might
otherwise have been attained.

B THE PARLOUR TAKES WHEELS

6 In the first twenty years of this century, the motor car was much 45
assailed as a threat to life and comfort, but rarely if ever as a menace
to morals.

7 Until the end of the First World War ninety per cent of motor cars
were roofless. Such closed cars as existed were slightly top-heavy
vehicles used by the wealthy as town carriages. The early motorists, 50
swathed in coats, scarves and rugs, goggled and veiled, and high-
perched in full view of the world, had other things to think of than
the call of the flesh. Their state of comfort was little higher than that
of their grandfathers, who had braved dust and sleet on the outside
of the stage-coach. But as soon as manufacturers began to put a roof 55
over motorists' heads, with the innocent idea of shielding them more
effectively from the weather, it was another story. The motor car

*Vanity Fair.

(like the hansom cab) became an intimate and exciting little box, and it is a basic if little-advertised human law that men and women cannot be tucked side by side into cosy little boxes without getting *60* ideas in their heads.

8   To the designer it was an engineering problem, pure and simple. If he roofed the vehicle, he must also lower the centre of gravity. How should he know that in doing so he was (as some have maintained) simultaneously lowering the standard of morality?   *65*

9   So far as this writer can discover, no manufacturer of motor cars ever advertised his roofed-in model as being ideally suited to the needs of courting couples. Cars, after all, were bought by fathers, who had no interest in providing amatory amenities for their young. Sinclair Lewis's Babbitt was badgered into buying a closed car *70* simply because it was the imperative new fashion. But there are some amenities which do not need to be advertised or advocated. In a startlingly brief space of time the closed car had done more to change the courting customs of the western world than any other agency, not excluding the cinema.   *75*

10   There were motor-car manufacturers who, in their innocence, prided themselves on having marketed something which would help to hold the family together, to give it a common interest; but sociologists were soon to see the automobile as an instrument for releasing youth from the tedious or tyrannical company of the old.   *80*

11   The trouble with the front parlour had been that parents exercised their right to sit there too, or to look in at frequent intervals. Younger brothers and sisters also wandered in, tiresomely. There was no question of being allowed to sit there in the dark. The closed car constituted a mobile parlour, excitingly shrunken in dimensions, *85* in which a couple were obliged to sit rather closer together than they normally would on the davenport; a parlour which could be driven away from the house and its occupants and halted at whim on a murmurous moonlit beach or in a leafy lane. Mobility, privacy and propinquity – never had Cupid been so well served. Sitting together *90* in a darkened car had much of the thrill of one of those hiding-in-the-cupboard games, except that there were all manner of adjuncts for comfort and convenience, ranging from electric light, mirror and foot-warmers to cigarette-lighter and (later) a radio set giving out sentimental music. And, of course, a flask in the door pocket, if the *95* couple had acquired the habit. The soft light from the dashboard shone downwards on a pair of long silk-stockinged legs. A very slight, and seemingly accidental, movement by the male leg was sufficient to establish contact, and if the first contact was not evaded successive contacts could be established. A girl could not be expected *100* to sit bolt upright when in a sentimental mood: the man's shoulder

was an inevitable support. It was all too easy. The only thing a man had to learn was to keep his elbow off the horn button. If the front seats were uncomfortable, or if the steering-wheel was in the way, there were always the back seats. Some cars had bench-type front *105* seats, the back of which lowered to blend, after a fashion, with the back seats. What was in the designer's mind is not clear, for if the intention had been to form a bed it could have been better designed. Even as it was, however, there were some young bloods who thought highly of this facility. *110*

12   Fathers and mothers were not ignorant of the risks attached to letting their children roam the countryside at will in a mobile parlour. Occasionally a parent would find a pretext for riding in the back seat, but the two-seater finally foiled the chaperon. In homes which contained only one living-room, no doubt there were fathers *115* who welcomed the chance to send the young couple away in a car, so that a man might emerge from exile in the kitchen and sit in a comfortable chair again.

From *A History of Courting*

=============

1 **a** What were the benefits of the chaperon system?

b (i) The chaperon hardly appears in Part B. What social changes are reflected by this change of emphasis?
(ii) 'The two-seater finally foiled the chaperon.' *(line 114)* What points are **implied** by this statement?

c Mention two or three points conveyed by the reference to the cinema *(line 75)*.

d One word you might expect is *not* found in these extracts. Say what you think it is and why the author does not use it.

2 **a** Analysis of the style, which is also part of the humour of the passage, reveals the following features:
(i) **alliteration** and **assonance**
(ii) **antithesis**
(iii) **formal** rather than **informal** expressions
(iv) **balance** of **syntax** or **structure**.

Which one or more of these is illustrated in:

    (i) 'that much misunderstood functionary' *(lines 1–2)*
    (ii) 'to preside in the parlour' *(line 7)*
    (iii) 'divine their intentions' *(line 11)*
    (iv) 'relished' *(line 32)*
    (v) 'consent' *(line 34)*
    (vi) 'neither duennas nor dupes' *(line 42)*
    (vii) 'much assailed as a threat to life and comfort, but rarely if ever as a menace to morals' *(lines 46–47)*
    (viii) 'amatory amenities'*(line 69)*
    (ix) 'mobility, privacy and propinquity' *(lines 89–90)*
    (x) 'adjuncts for comfort and convenience' *(lines 92–93)*?

b Humour of a different kind seems to spring from items like:

    (i) 'flirtatious chaperons' *(lines 39–40)*
    (ii) 'a mobile parlour' *(line 85)*
    (iii) 'The only thing a man had to learn was to keep his elbow off the horn button' *(lines 102–103)*
    (iv) 'a man might emerge from exile' *(line 117)*.

Try to identify the humorous element in these.

3 a Would the Victorian girl have welcomed the change from her own parlour to the 'parlour on wheels'?

b Would you agree that the engineer was 'simultaneously lowering the standard of morality' *(line 65)*?

c At the end of the book the author discusses some comments on courting today. Give your views on one or more of them:

'Courting needs a new code of manners, a new fastidiousness. There is too much mauling. Social intercourse between the sexes needs to be enlivened, as it once was, by grace, courtesy, fascination and wit.'

'Courting is in a rut. Couples rarely look for mates outside their immediate social class. The result is social inbreeding of the worst kind.'

'Courting couples 'rush into' marriage without being instructed or trained for it, without even exchanging medical certificates.'

23 The Sexes are Really Different
Benjamin Spock

Dr Spock became internationally known with his *Baby and Child Care* (1945), which sold twenty-eight million copies. Other books include *Talks with Mothers* (1962) and *Problems of Parents* (1963). *Decent and Indecent* analyses the problems of western society including disillusionment, sex roles, aggression, political attitudes and education.

1 You can't tell whether there are innate temperamental differences between the sexes by determining what is the typical or normal role for man or for woman. Man has been a cruel warrior, a lace-trimmed dandy, a monk, a scientist. Woman has been a plodding farmer, a dancing girl, a novelist, even a bullfighter in ancient Crete. There are 5
tribes where the only thing that the men do is to trade shells or carve gourds, while the women carry out all the jobs that keep body and soul together. And there have been societies in which a man rich enough to have servants could afford a wife who was only an ornament. 10
2 I realise that the question of innate differences is a highly controversial one and that some experts deny there is any such thing. What follows are my own observations of differences that I believe are at least partly innate though they may be accentuated or obscured by culture and family upbringing. 15
3 Very few girls right from birth seem to have as much striving and restlessness as the average boy. Even at one year of age I think boys have a greater interest in mechanical objects that can be investigated and manipulated. Girls as toddlers are more compliant than boys; they can be toilet trained more easily. More girls get high grades at 20
school and college, because they are inclined to accept the instructor's word as long as it is reasonable. Boys have a tendency to question and argue, openly or silently, which often keeps them from even hearing what the instructor is saying. Women on the average are more ready to make the multiple adjustments of marriage. With 25
eyes wide open they will overlook the imperfections and absurdities of their husbands, provided their husbands love and need them. A considerable majority of women when they marry join the same political party as their husbands; this doesn't mean that they have

95

any less capacity for analysis or opinion but that their devotion to 30
their husbands disposes them to see their husbands' point of view.

4   Women are usually more patient in working at unexciting,
repetitive tasks. Women working at a soda fountain simply make
sandwiches and drinks. Men must turn such an occupation into a
system, a combination of game, ballet, and race against time in 35
which they grab the bread, slap on the filling, slice, and sling the
sandwich – all in one rapid, sleight-of-hand movement – meanwhile
bellowing cryptic orders back and forth and slipping exaggerated
compliments to their female customers.

5   Women on the average have more passivity in the inborn core of 40
their personality, though this can be counteracted and hidden from
view when they are brought up in an atmosphere that encourages
aggressiveness. The pattern of women's greater instinctive passivity
is evident in sexual relations. Girls and women who are up against
male indifference can be boldly provocative, as in the case of 45
fourteen- and fifteen-year-old girls who will pursue the bashful boys
of this age but quiet down if and when older, more masterful boys
become interested. Women involved with men who clam up or are
meek will sometimes get wildly provocative with taunts, to make
them angry and aggressive. But these kinds of provocation are to 50
serve a passive need.

6   Boys and men have potentially much more aggressiveness, though
this can be thoroughly controlled and curbed by upbringing. Even at
two or three years they sense the general spirit of pistol play, long
before they have any knowledge of death or ballistics. They continue 55
to play cowboy or soldier with sparkling eyes and barking guns until
they are nearly adolescent, an occupation that very few girls can be
drawn into even briefly.

7   Young girls at an ice rink skate sociably with each other or
practise twirls before the mirror. Boys of this age persistently and 60
illegally skate against the current and play tag in and out amongst
the nervous adults, enjoying the combat with each other and the
indignation of the older people.

8   Erik Erikson in a revealing experiment presented small dolls
representing adults and children, dolls' furniture, toy cars, building 65
blocks to a series of American school-age boys and girls. He asked
each one to set the stage and indicate a scenario for a movie about an
exciting occurrence. Boys built towering structures with the blocks –
a characteristic assertion of manliness – and then usually depicted a
scene of violence, most commonly a burglary or a traffic accident. 70
Policemen were used frequently, to arrest the culprit of a burglary or
collision. Boys are preoccupied with aggression but equally with the
need to control it.

9   Girls would use the blocks, if at all, to outline the rooms in a house. They would arrange the furniture by rooms. Then they placed *75* members of the family in conventional domestic situations. A typical drama consisted of the two parents sitting in the living room listening while their daughter played the piano for them!

10   I suppose that if the girl had been reminded again, towards the end of her stage-setting, that the theme was to be an exciting event, she *80* would have been able to substitute something more dramatic than piano-playing. But the significant thing was, I think, that by the time she had created the household plan she had forgotten that the drama was meant to be exciting and simply followed her temperamental inclination.   *85*

11   The emotional strengths that women contribute to family life in our society are realism, discernment, the personal touch. They sense clearly the human relationships around them. They have a strong urge to satisfy human needs. They enjoy making people comfortable. They sympathise with those who are suffering. (Suffering people *90* make quite a few men acutely uncomfortable and impatient.) These qualities make women indispensable as wives, mothers, nurses, secretaries.

12   Women are not fascinated with gadgets for their own sake; they view them sceptically until they prove their utility. They see a car as *95* simply transport; they have no craving to buy a particular one because it is new-fangled or powerful; they generally object to the foolishness of spending extra money for such qualities.

.   .   .   .   .   .

13   The most valuable quality that men contribute to their family or organisation or community is their ability to analyse a problem – to *100* focus on one particular aspect of it, work out the theory behind it, find some kind of general solution. This is how they become, more often than women, inventors, discoverers, builders. More easily than women they can shut out the wholeness and the human realities of a situation in order to define an underlying abstraction. The dis-*105* advantage of this ability, for family life, is the tendency of many men to be somewhat absent-minded and impersonal. Girls can also be made impersonal but it takes much more mental disciplining by sternly intellectual parents and teachers to suppress their feelings.

From *Decent and Indecent*

1 a A key idea in the passage is carried by the word 'innate' in paragraphs 1 and 2. Find the word in paragraph 2 which is in **opposition** to it.

b Divide the following items, some from the passage, into two groups:

(i) those that broadly belong with 'innate'
(ii) those in opposition to it:

'role' *(line 2)*, 'societies' *(line 8)*, 'family upbringing' *(line 15)*, 'inborn' *(line 40)*, 'instinctive' *(line 43)*, 'conventional' *(line 76)*, learning, acquired characteristics, genetic, nature, nurture, environment, custom, heredity, racial, training.

c Into which group, (i) or (ii), would you put the following:

speaking, the sex urge, aggression, sleeping, self-defence, curiosity, love?

d (i) Make two columns, M and F, and list the features which Dr Spock says are typical of males and females, e.g.

M	F
striving	compliant
restlessness	amenable to instruction
etc.	etc.

(ii) Say which two points in the list you find most, and which two least, convincing. Give reasons.

2 a Erik Erickson's experiment *(paragraphs 8, 9 and 10)* is open to certain objections. Say what these are.

b Devise another experiment to show whether there are differences of temperament between the sexes.

c (i) Later in the chapter Dr Spock lists other characteristics typical of each sex. Deduce the sex to which he would ascribe these:

A readiness to change one's mind
B fear of losing face
C reluctance to publicly admit a mistake

D   fear of not being accorded authority
E   tendency to personalise an impersonal situation
F   compulsion to confront danger
G   readiness to ask for help
H   bowing to custom and obligation
I   competitive driving.

(ii) Invent situations illustrating *two* of these characteristics.

3 a Suggest one **implication** Dr Spock's ideas would have, if correct, for *three* of the following:

(i) girls' education (ii) the driving test (iii) a happy marriage (iv) women at work (v) 'women's lib' (vi) children's toys (vii) children's literature.

24 The Great Male Plot
Casey Miller and Kate Swift

Casey Miller became a publisher's assistant in New York, a career to which she returned after service in the US Navy in the Second World War, becoming acting director of publications for Colonial Williamsburg Inc. in Virginia, and later, Curriculum Editor at the Seabury Press.

Kate Swift served in the US Army and worked as a reporter, as a science writer and editor for the American Museum of Natural History and the Yale University School of Medicine.

In 1970 Miller and Swift formed a freelance editorial team. While copy editing a school sex education course they found that 'whatever the authors' intentions, the message coming through was that girls are not as important, responsible or self-sufficient as boys or as healthy in their outlook on life'. This led Miller and Swift to think about 'the sexist nature of accepted English usage' and eventually to write *Words and Women*.

Trevor Fishlock, since 1980 in the Foreign Department of *The Times*, has had a varied career in journalism. He has a special interest in Welsh affairs. His book *Wales and the Welsh* was published in 1972, *Talking of Wales* in 1975 and *Wales* in 1979. After spending nine months on a travelling scholarship in the USA he wrote *Americans and Nothing Else* in 1980. His view, conflicting with those of Casey Miller and Kate Swift, is given on page 104.

---

1   The male bias of English did not have to be fostered by a conspiracy. It came about through the working of a familiar principle: power tends to corrupt. English is male-oriented because it evolved through centuries of patriarchy to meet the needs of patriarchy. Those in power tend to try to stay there, and those out of power, to make the   *5* best of what they are allotted. But because women's image of themselves is changing, language is changing in response. Generations of women, taught to value the accomplishments of their husbands (or fathers or brothers or sons) more highly than their own, made an emotional investment in being identified through   *10* males. However, once enough wives, daughters, sisters and mothers began to say, 'But I have my own identity,' new wheels were set in motion, new life-styles began to appear, and new linguistic symbols emerged to describe them. All of which can be seen in the recent history of women's social titles.   *15*

2   The abbreviation Ms has been around as a title of courtesy since at least the 1940s, but it was largely unused until two things happened:

the growth of direct mail selling made the abbreviation an effective time and money saver, and a significant number of women began to object to being labelled according to their (presumed) marital status. *20*

3   The 1972 *American Heritage School Dictionary* was the first dictionary to include Ms, which it defined as 'an abbreviation used as a title of courtesy before a woman's last name or before her given name and last name, whether she is married or not'. By 1976 dictionaries published by Merriam-Webster, Random House, *25* Doubleday, Funk and Wagnalls and Collins-World also included Ms as an accepted social form analogous to Mr.

4   The opposition to Ms has been intense and emotional, however. The arguments that it cannot be pronounced, that it has an ugly sound, or that it is not a true abbreviation are often offered with a *30* vehemence not justified by their merit. Is it possible to tell by looking at Mr and Mrs that they are pronounced mister and missiz (or mizz in some parts of the country)? Is the sibilant in Ms any more disagreeable to the ear than the hiss in Miss? For sheer silliness of sound one would be hard pressed to beat the long-accepted plural *35* form of Mr, commonly if inelegantly pronounced messers. Finally, is Ms any less true an abbreviation than Miss or Mrs? If the problem is guilt by association with the opprobrious *mistress*, all three titles must share it.

5   In its earliest meaning mistress described a woman, either married *40* or unmarried, who had authority over servants, children or a household. It was a prestigious word, like master, and when prefixed to a woman's name was a title of respect. Some time in the seventeenth century the noun mistress and its written abbreviations Mis, Miss and Mrs, acquired the additional meaning of concubine *45* and occasionally of prostitute. The only forms to escape this association were apparently those prefixed to proper names as courtesy titles, and these eventually acquired their own pronunciation distinct from mistress. In this period, Mrs was applied to all adult women, Miss to female children. Among other examples, the *50* *Oxford English Dictionary* cites Samuel Pepys' diary entry of 1666, 'Little Miss Davis did dance a jigg after the end of the play,' and Tobias Smollett's observation of 1751 that 'Mrs Grizzle . . . was now in the thirtieth year of her maidenhood.'

6   By the beginning of the nineteenth century, however, the titles *55* were no longer being used to distinguish children from adults. They had become labels identifying marital status: Mrs distinguished married women and the 'infantine term *miss*', as it was characterised in H J Todd's 1818 edition of Johnson's dictionary, was applied to unmarried adult women as well as to children.   *60*

7   No comprehensive study has been made of what prompted this

change, but the timing strongly suggests a connection with women's increasing participation in the Industrial Revolution. This period was one of social ferment. Up to the time that large numbers of women left their homes to work in the new industries, the ordinary 65 woman's primary identity had been that of daughter or wife/mother. She lived and worked under the roof of the man who ruled her person – her father or husband – and her relationship to him was apparent or easily learned. Once women gained a measure of independence as paid labourers, these ties were obscured and 70 loosened. A man could not tell by looking at a woman spinning cotton in a textile mill to whom she 'belonged' or whether she was 'available'.

8   Under these circumstances a simple means of distinguishing married from unmarried women was needed (by men) and it served a 75 double purpose: it supplied at least a modicum of information about a woman's sexual availability, and it applied not-so-subtle social pressure towards marriage by lumping single women with the young and inexperienced. Attached to anyone over the age of about eighteen, Miss came in time to suggest the unattractive or socially 80 undesirable qualities associated with such labels as 'old maid' and 'spinster' or the dreadful word *barren*. So the needs of patriarchy were served when a woman's availability for her primary role as helper and sexual partner was made an integral part of her identity – in effect, a part of her name.   85

From *Words and Women*

1 a The extract could be divided into two main sections. Say where the division would come and make a brief **summary** of the contents of each part.

   b If this extract were anonymous, we might guess the writer(s) to be female. How?

   c (i) State or find out the meaning of 'patriarchy' (*line 4*).
      (ii) Find the points in paragraphs 2, 5, 7 and 8 which relate to this idea.

   d Some women might object to 'Ms' for reasons other than those given in paragraph 4. Suggest some points they might make.

2 a Do you agree that 'Ms' is **analogous** to 'Mr'? *(line 27)* Give reasons.

b Which single words would be, in your opinion, most closely **synonymous** with:

'conspiracy' *(line 1)* 'corrupt' *(line 3)* 'evolved' *(line 3)* 'accomplishments' *(line 8)* 'vehemence' *(line 31)* 'sibilant' *(line 33)* 'opprobrious' *(line 38)* 'distinguish' *(line 56)* 'characterised' *(line 58)* 'integral' *(line 84)*?

c (i) Say which meanings best fit the phrases given:

A 'emotional investment' *(line 10)* self-image
B 'marital status' *(line 20)* shameful connection
C 'guilt by association' *(line 38)* chief part to play
D 'social ferment' *(line 64)* rewarding commitment
E 'primary identity' *(line 66)* position defined by marriage
F 'primary role' *(line 83)* important changes in thought and behaviour

(ii) Write a **paragraph** setting one of the phrases in a new context.

d (i) Of the arguments in lines 31–39, three are implied by questions and two carried by statements. Say briefly what the arguments are and into which one or more of these **categories** they fall, in your view:

Relevant   Irrelevant   True   Untrue   Strong   Weak

(ii) Devise a chart incorporating the categories in (i) above.
(iii) 'Power tends to corrupt.' *(lines 2–3)* Invent some arguments on this topic and say where they would come in your chart.

3 a (i) State the case for devising courtesy titles for bachelors, married men and widowers.
(ii) Invent suitable titles for the three categories.

b Give

(i) your opinion
(ii) what you imagine might be the opinion of Casey Miller and Kate Swift on this item from *The Times* (Trevor Fishlock's 'London Diary' for 29 January 1980):

A wider audience should know that *The Times* is making an historic stand on a matter of public interest. As now announced in a supplement to *The Times* style book, that forlorn fatherless and motherless little word Ms is cast into the lexicographical outer darkness.

Our style book is a small blue volume which guides us in our daily grappling with the language. I dare say some of my colleagues read a comforting page or two at bedtime. Indeed, it is such an interesting little book that I would not be surprised if it had some commercial potential . . .

The style book says that Ms is not an acceptable substitute for Miss or Mrs (except in certain special circumstances).

This is a rallying point for commonsense. There are several reasons why Ms should be allowed no air. It is artificial, ugly, silly, means nothing and is rotten English. It is a faddish middle-class plaything; and far from disguising the marital status of women, as is claimed, it draws attention to it. It is a vanity.

But, worst of all, those who stamp their petulant feet and insist on its use have lost sight of the ball. There *is* an important battle to be fought for all women, not just a tiny elite. And while the Msers are straining at gnats the struggle is elsewhere. Like chairperson, and the dotty battle for the dubious 'right' to stand next to plump lawyers in El Vino, Ms is one of the excesses of the revolution and should be junked. Such pursuit of the inconsequential will only end in tears.

That's torn it, I suppose. But in the end I can't be too hard on *les belles femmes*, even those who talk libberish. Underneath they're all lovable.

25 A Race of Thinking Animals?
Edwin Muir

Edwin Muir was born in 1887 and lived in the Orkneys until he was fourteen; some of his poetry reflects the emotions of these early years. He worked as office clerk in various industrial concerns and married Willa Anderson in 1919. The pair travelled widely in Europe and translated many German writers, including Kafka. Muir later worked for the British Council in Rome and as Warden of Newbattle Abbey College, Scotland. His *Collected Poems* were published in 1952. He died in 1959.

1 I do not have the power to prove that man is immortal and that the soul exists; but I know that there must be such a proof, and that compared with it every other demonstration is idle. It is true that human life without immortality would be inconceivable to me, though that is not the ground for my belief. It would be incon- 5 ceivable because if man is an animal by direct descent I can see human life only as a nightmare populated by animals wearing top-hats and kid gloves, painting their lips and touching up their cheeks and talking in heated rooms, rubbing their muzzles together in the moment of lust, going through innumerable clever tricks, learning to 10 make and listen to music, to gaze sentimentally at sunsets, to count, to acquire a sense of humour, to give their lives for some cause, or to pray.

2   This picture has always been in my mind since one summer evening in Glasgow in 1919. I did not believe in the immortality of 15 the soul at that time; I was deep in the study of Nietzsche, and had cast off with a great sense of liberation all belief in any other life than the life we live here and now, as an imputation on the purity of immediate experience, which I had intellectually convinced myself was guiltless and beyond good and evil. I was returning in a tramcar 20 from my work; the tramcar was full and very hot; the sun burned through the glass on backs of necks, shoulders, faces, trousers, skirts, hands, all stacked there impartially. Opposite me was sitting a man with a face like a pig's, and as I looked at him in the oppressive heat the words came into my mind, 'That is an animal.' I looked round me 25 at the other people in the tramcar; I was conscious that something had fallen from them and from me; and with a sense of desolation I saw that they were all animals, some of them good, some evil, some

charming, some sad, some happy, some sick, some well. The tramcar
stopped and went on again, carrying its menagerie; my mind saw *30*
countless other tramcars where animals sat or got on or off with
mechanical dexterity, as if they had been trained in a circus; and I
realized that in all Glasgow, in all Scotland, in all the world, there
was nothing but millions of such creatures living an animal life and
moving towards an animal death as towards a great slaughter-house. *35*
I stared at the faces, trying to make them human again and to dispel
the hallucination, but I could not. This experience was so terrifying
that I dismissed it, deliberately forgot it by that perverse power
which the mind has of obliterating itself. I felt as if I had lived for a
few moments in Swift's world, for Swift's vision of humanity was the *40*
animal vision. I could not have endured it for more than a few
minutes. I did not associate it at the time with Nietzsche. But I
realised that I could not bear mankind as a swarming race of
thinking animals, and that if there was not somewhere, it did not
matter where – in a suburb of Glasgow or of Hong Kong or of *45*
Honolulu – a single living soul, life was a curious, irrelevant
desolation. I pushed away this realization for a time, but it returned
again later, like the memory of my cowardice as a boy.

From *An Autobiography*

1 **a** Select a word or phrase from the first paragraph which would
serve as an alternative title to the extract.

   b What do you deduce were Nietzsche's views on this life and the
after-life *(lines 15–20)*?

   c The words 'some of them good, some evil' *(line 28)* raise a
philosophical problem. Can you say what it is?

2 **a** Find two **similes** and two **metaphors** in paragraph 2 by which
Edwin Muir emphasises the idea of man as an animal.

   b Show how the word 'but' *(line 42)* introduces a turning point in
the writer's argument.

3   What comment would (a) Edwin Muir (b) you   make on these
remarks by Desmond Morris?

The modern human animal is no longer living in conditions natural for his species. Trapped, not by a zoo collector, but by his own brainy brilliance, he has set himself up in a huge, restless menagerie where he is in constant danger of cracking under the strain.

From *The Human Zoo*

26 Death Wish Without Pride

Geoffrey Robertson

Geoffrey Robertson sent the following note on his career: I am a barrister who
has appeared in a number of cases involving civil rights, such as the *Gay News*
blasphemy case, the 'ABC' Official Secrets trial and the *New Statesman*
contempt case. I am also an author, whose works include *Reluctant Judas*
(Temple-Smith, 1976), *Obscenity* (Weidenfeld, 1979), and several forthcoming
books on press freedom. I am currently Visiting Fellow in Law at Warwick
University, an executive member of the Defence of Literature and the Arts
Society, and editor of *The Guardian's* 'Out of Court' column.

1 The bodies of suicides were once buried by night at crossroads, with
a stake through their hearts and a stone on their heads. In 1961, to the
discomfort only of insurance companies, self-murder ceased to be a
crime and survivors could no longer be prosecuted for botching their
own demise. Yet the compassionate doctor who, even by request,   *5*
shortens the life of a dying patient remains guilty of murder, and
anyone else who dares to help or advise a sufferer set on suicide
commits an offence punishable by fourteen years imprisonment. In
other words we have the right to die, but not with dignity. The law
permits sucide, but does its best to ensure that the job will be bungled.   *10*
2 'The law', in this context, is a euphemism for the Director of
Public Prosecutions, whose consent is necessary before any prosecution can be brought for aiding and abetting suicide. Usually, he
tries to look the other way. Medical decisions to hasten death have
scarcely been questioned since the acquittal of John Bodkin Adams,   *15*
although the strict letter of the law still stays the hand of most
sympathetic doctors.
3   The mercy killer's anguish shames the penal system, and is kept
out of court whenever possible: not even Derek Humphrey's detailed
public confession of how he assisted his wife's suicide (*Jean's Way*)   *20*
could provoke a prosecution. But suddenly, all has changed: police
are making arrests, interrogating journalists and badgering TV
companies for interviews filmed with euthanasia counsellors and
their victims. This activity by Scotland Yard is apparently to prepare
the ground for trials which will entangle the criminal law with new   *25*
problems of free will and free speech.

4   There are those who believe it is best to let sleeping laws lie, instead of unleashing them upon actions sincerely and painfully taken in response to private tragedy. But bad laws are never justified on the grounds that they will be sensibly administered, and the subject of 30 euthanasia calls for careful distinctions which neither the present law nor those who enforce it are capable of making. There can be dignity in the decision to die, and decency in assisting it, which calls for neither condemnation nor punishment.

5   In Sir Thomas More's *Utopia*, priests and magistrates were 35 obliged to counsel the incurably ill towards an 'honorable death.' After proper inquiry, a citizen was entitled to 'either despatch himself out of that painful life, as out of a prison or a rack of torment, or else suffer himself willingly to be rid out of it by other.' The law, however, took its cue from Blackstone, who condemned the 40 suicide for the spiritual presumption of 'invading the prerogative of the Almighty, and rushing into his immediate presence uncalled for.'

6   The judges, when they first came to rule on suicide in the sixteenth century, added a more feudal reason; it was a crime against the king, because it deprived him of a valuable subject and set a bad example 45 to other vassals. The Suicide Act of 1961 abolished the old crime but perpetuated punishment for any person 'who aids, abets, counsels or procures the suicide of another or an attempt by another to commit suicide' (Section Two).

7   The practical effect of this law is that you can kill yourself if you 50 can. This is a difficult operation for the bedridden, and an unreliable excercise for those who adopt familiar methods, like wrist-slitting or drug overdosing. There are, however, several fool-proof ways of despatching oneself, cleanly and comfortably.

8   These methods may not be published without danger of infringing 55 Section Two, and it may even be an offence to explain them to those determined to take their own life. The Suicide Act, in short, places an embargo upon advice or assistance offered with the intention of easing death. Doctors, relatives and counsellors must turn a deaf ear to the pleas of sufferers racked with cancer (although the law permits 60 cigarette manufacturers to traffic with impunity).

9   Why should those who deliberately and calmly choose to die be denied some simple facts, and some ordinary drugs, with which to effectuate their choice? At present, because the law which denies them these rights is the only safeguard against the greed of a Yolande 65 McShane, the mass hysteria of Jonestown and the instability of transient emotions.

10   No civilised society could countenance the artful persuasion of the aged, to die for the benefit of their testators, or permit religious or other cranks to manipulate death wishes. Section Two of the Act 70

properly punishes such presumptions. And I doubt whether many latter day Voltairians would really defend to their own death the publication of a do-it-yourself guide to successful suicide, available at W H Smith's for any temporarily depressed teenager to pluck up the courage that his unaided imagination would baulk at. 75

11 Distinctions must be drawn, before the enthusiastic euthanasiast becomes a social menace.

12 How can the law be changed to reflect these distinctions? The Parliamentary supporters of voluntary euthanasia have promoted several bills in recent years, which have foundered upon drafting 80 difficulties and the feeling that the moral dilemmas of suicide are best left to doctors and the DPP. But laws which make murderers of doctors who agree to extinguish intolerable lives, and which permit a public official to prosecute those whose actions may genuinely relieve suffering, only deepen the moral dilemma. 85

13 Sir Thomas More's Utopian solution to the right to an officially sanctioned demise on proof of anguish and incurability, worked for Tom Conti in the play *Whose Life Is It Anyway?*, but there might be real life difficulties – notably delay – in requiring every potential suicide to brief counsel to apply for a judicial declaration of fitness 90 for an assisted death.

14 A simpler solution would be to amend Section Two of the Suicide Act so that it would apply only to those who 'without legitimate reason' aid or abet suicide. These three simple words supply what Lord Scarman recently described in another context as 'a highly re- 95 spectable and dignified defence.' That seems exactly right for those whose highly respectable and dignified actions are currently punishable by up to fourteen years in prison.

From *The Guardian* 21 July 1980

1 a How do you interpret the title of this article? (The end of paragraph 1 might give a clue.)

b Is the general aim of the article

(i) to defend euthanasia, or
(ii) to criticise the law on suicide?

c What arguments are stated in

(i) lines 40–42 (ii) lines 43–46;
and **implied** in (iii) lines 50–53 (iv) lines 59–60?
(v) Say why you would support or reject any *one* of these arguments.

2 a   (i) What is a 'euphemism' *(line 11)*?
(ii) Check the **derivation** of 'euphemism' and 'euthanasia' *(line 23)* to find the link between the two words.
(iii) Does the word 'Utopia' *(line 35)* have the same link?

b   The article contains a number of **explicit** references (e.g. to books like *Jean's Way (line 20)* and *Utopia (line 35))* and **allusions** (e.g. to Voltaire *(line 72)*, who said 'I disapprove of what you say, but I will defend to the death your right to say it').

Explain or deduce the **allusions** to
John Bodkin Adams *(line 15)* Blackstone *(line 40)* Yolande McShane *(lines 65–66)* Jonestown *(line 66)* W H Smith's *(line 74)* Tom Conti *(line 88)* Lord Scarman *(lines 94–95)*.

3   What are the pros and cons of the 'simple solution' suggested in the last paragraph?

27 Euthanasia
F. R. Barry

The Rt Revd F. R. Barry was Bishop of Southwell for twenty-two years, having also held academic posts at Oxford and London Universities and a Canonry of Westminster. His books (e.g. *Christianity and Psychology; The Relevance of Christianity; Asking the Right Questions*) show concern with the role of the Church in Society. The book from which the extract is taken deals with such matters as 'Charity and Chastity', 'God and Caesar', 'Morals and the Law' and 'The Affluent Society'.

1 The religious condemnation of suicide seems to rest fundamentally on the argument that our lives belong to God, not to ourselves. We violate the sanctity of life if we cast it away by our own act. That is not for us to decide; we must abide our going hence even as our coming hither. I have tried to appraise the Christian attitude and 5 have inclined to a more lenient judgement than every reader may be prepared to endorse. But what if, instead of taking his own life when he is in the grip of a painful illness, the patient asks the doctor to do it for him? (In practice there will normally be an abettor. Someone must put the means within his reach.) Or if the doctor quietly lets him 10 die when he knows that he is beyond human aid? It would seem that the problem of euthanasia is really an extension of the same problem which has been discussed in the previous pages. It involves much the same moral principles and many of the same legal questions. The problem arises not from human wickedness but from two things that 15 are essentially good – first from the advance of medical techniques and then from one of our best moral assets, the magnificent ethical code of the Profession. And here too informed public opinion, and within it Christian opinion, is on the move. Does the Hippocratic oath, reinforced by Christian tradition, necessitate, and does the 20 sanctity of human life imply, that it is in all cases a moral duty to keep men alive to the last possible moment? And in view of the latest medical techniques we must ask what exactly is meant by 'alive'?

2   The doctor is the servant of life. He labours with dedicated devotion, often against nearly impossible odds, to fight off death and 25 preserve his patient's life. And the trust of the patient and the relatives is based on the knowledge that he will never desist from

that. (It is true, we are told, that any skilful doctor could kill a patient without trace if he wished and that there could be no legal protection. But such is the great professional tradition that no one would ever 30 imagine the possibility. The patient knows that the doctor is on his side.) But is there a point when that obligation ceases? In an intolerably painful illness for which there is no possibility of cure, so that it is certainly going to end in death, is he morally bound to prevent the man from dying for one more day or for one more hour 35 up to the very last extreme moment? If pneumonia meanwhile supervenes, is he morally bound to administer antibiotics? If the patient himself asks to be released from what has become little more than a living death, may he justifiably give him his quietus? Does the sanctity of life mean that the prolongation of physical existence, 40 under any conditions and at any price, is an absolute, incommensurable value, or can there be a standard of valuation which is qualitative rather than merely quantitative? If physical death is the worst thing that can happen to us then presumably it is a moral duty to subordinate everything else to its postponement. But that is not a 45 Christian valuation. There is a Christian attitude to death as well as a Christian attitude to life.

3   Morally, it may seem unrealistic to describe it as murder if a patient is released from life by his own expressed wish. But the law as it now stands is quite uncompromising. If anyone gives the patient a 50 tablet which he knowingly takes and then dies, that is murder. (It is the same crime as abetting suicide.) In such charges consent is no defence. And still more obviously if the other party has given and is proved to have given a fatal dose or injection, that is murder. The doctor has no immunity from that law. On general grounds 55 Christians will support all measures that tend to the safeguarding of life, and they would, I think, rightly resist any proposed changes in the present law which would confer immunity in such cases on anyone other than the patient's doctor. But this is the doctor's position at the moment. It is true, no doubt, that the charge is very 60 seldom brought, though the police may at any time be forced to bring it, and that in practice the judge's direction may allow the substitution of a lower charge or may involve the doctrine of necessity or that the jury may refuse to convict. But the full legal consequences *may* fall on him. And the logical implications of the 65 present law, if strictly applied, may even be found to militate against the anaesthetisation of pain.

4   When a patient is in great agony the minimum dose required to kill the pain may in fact be one that is likely to prove fatal. Is a doctor to be prevented from giving it by the threat of having to face a charge of 70 murder? Again, as a patient becomes habituated to narcotic drugs

they may have to be administered in progressively increasing doses, and the time will come when the choice will have to be made between leaving the patient's agony unrelieved and relieving it but by shortening his life or at least by accelerating his death. Few will 75 doubt what the decision ought to be. Yet the doctor *has*, in effect, 'killed' the patient.

5   Moral theologians justify the decision under the doctrine of double effect and the law may rely on the doctrine of necessity. But how far is there any real moral difference between the deliberate 80 giving of a dose knowing that it will in fact prove fatal and deliberately giving a fatal dose?

6   The withholding of medical means to prolong life – not striving officiously to keep alive – seems to raise no moral problems, and is said by authorities to be 'probably lawful'. The phrase commonly 85 used in this context is the distinction between the prolongation of life and the prolongation of the act of dying. But the phrase does not really cover the facts. Death and life are no longer so clearly distinguishable. *When* does a man die? When his heart stops beating? The use of electronics in cardiac surgery brings the whole 90 problem into a new phase. It is possible to keep a man 'alive', that is to say to keep his heart beating, long after consciousness has been destroyed, with no possible hope of recovery, by brain injury. I have known of a case that lasted two years, and one of even twelve years has been reported. How far can this be called life? If the doctor 95 switches off the machine can he really be said to have 'killed' that poor body in which the spirit's self had ceased to burn? Can there possibly be any moral obligation to prolong that physical existence and indeed can it even be morally right to do it? Can the sanctity of life require that?   100

7   Here it may be repeated that for the Christian there is a value in death as well as in life. For those who share the Christian hope death is a gate into life: *mors ianua vitae*. But for all men, Christians and others, death is a relevant fact of human life and indeed the inescapable condition of it. There is a time to live and a time to die. 105 When that time comes the enemy comes as a friend and the patient should not be held back from joining him.

8   Christian opinion, in its official expressions, is at present very strongly opposed to any legalising of euthanasia. It is probable, too, that majority opinion in this country and in most other countries 110 would oppose it. No country has in fact yet taken that step. It might result in making life cheap. It might result in all manner of abuses. If suicide ceases to be a crime then it would not be an offence for *anybody* to put the poison into the patient's hand, and that gap

would have to be stopped accordingly. There is probably no *115* responsible opinion that would contemplate unrestricted euthanasia. It would have to be rigorously confined to the doctor and perhaps also to cases of terminal illness. I do not think that with those limitations and those safeguards Christian opinion need resist a liberalisation of the law. Everyone knows that doctors do in fact *120* give drugs that have the effect of shortening life and everyone approves of their doing it — would indeed censure them if they failed to do it. Every day they have to make decisions which involve terrible responsibility in the secret places of their conscience in the light of their own best medical judgement. Public opinion trusts them *125* implicitly. We all put our lives in the doctor's hands. Why should we think that he will become less trustworthy if he is given legal protection?

9   In a House of Lords debate the Archbishop of Canterbury (Lang) argued, and Lord Horder had given the lead, that the right way of *130* dealing with the question was to suggest no new legislation and not to propose any legalising, but to leave everything where it is in practice, that is, within the discretion of the doctor. Most opinion, Christian or other, would probably at the moment agree with that. But it is most unfair to the doctor, and in the long run also to the *135* patient, to deprive him of protection under the law. He cannot make an objective professional judgement if the threat, however remote, of prosecution or blackmail is sitting on his shoulder. The case could be met by a measure which would not give a patient a right to euthanasia nor be dependent on the consent of relatives (who may *140* have an interest in the death) but would provide protection to the doctor in the exercise of his professional judgement. (He might decide to refuse the patient's request.) It might simply provide that it is not an offence for a qualified medical practitioner to accelerate the death of a patient who is suffering from severe pain in an incurable *145* and fatal illness unless it is proved that the act was not done in good faith and with the patient's consent. The doctor would have to prove the medical facts. It would be for the Crown to prove bad faith.

From *Christian Ethics and Secular Society*

1 a The passage is concerned with both 'moral' and 'legal' questions.

    (i) **Define** each word.

    (ii) Invent situations (*not* concerned with the topic of the passage) where a moral action is illegal and where a legal action is immoral.

  b What according to the author is the Christian attitude to (i) life (ii) death (iii) euthanasia?

  c Hippocrates, a Greek physician, formulated his famous oath about 400 BC. Say whether you would 'update' this part of it and, if so, how: 'The regimen I adopt shall be for the benefit of my patients according to my ability and judgment and not for their hurt or any wrong. I will give no deadly drug to any, though it be asked me, nor will I counsel such.'

2 a (i) Say what answers you would give to the questions in lines 32–43.

    (ii) What is the writer's purpose in including these questions?

    (iii) What different purpose lies behind the question in line 89?

  b How and why does the author **qualify** his statements about Christian opinion in lines 117–120 and lines 133–134?

3 a What is the difference between the proposal made in lines 138–148 and the solution offered by Geoffrey Robertson in paragraph 14 of the preceding extract?

  b Say with reasons whether you would support the Barry or Robertson (page 110) solution, or neither.

28 Changes in Working Class Life

Richard Hoggart

Richard Hoggart became well-known when he published *The Uses of Literacy* (1957) – a survey, including a backward look at his own working-class childhood, of the culture and attitudes of 'the masses'. Hoggart has been involved with the teaching of literature throughout his professional life and was Professor of English at Birmingham University from 1962–73. He has been connected with numerous bodies concerned with the Arts (e.g. the British Council, the Pilkington Committee on Broadcasting, UNESCO and the Royal Shakespeare Theatre). He is now Warden of Goldsmith's College, London University.

1 I should guess that it is a long time since British people as a whole, and working-class people in particular, felt so sharply the sense of change in their lives. This conversation was recorded in a public-house in a Northern working-class district at the beginning of the 1960s. I do not think one would have heard it five years before. It 5
indicates with economy, and vividly, the main cause and effect of the changes in British life today. The speaker is a middle-aged working-man:

'Everyone's bloody-upside-down if you ask me,' said Freddy. 10
'They're bound to be happier,' went on Owd Jem, 'because they've
got a bit of cash to play with!' He stared at us to let his words sink in.
'Before the war money was that tight every penny was spoken for!
But today folk have a bit of choice. And they feel better for it. You go
out and you can see it on their faces. They're no longer frightened. 15
They feel freer. It stands to reason!'*

Prosperity – to make generalisations out of what he is saying – removes old fears and increases confidence; it increases the power to make choices of one's own, because the straitjacket of poverty has been loosened. It increases the feeling of individuality, of being a person with idiosyncratic wishes and decisions. Of course, to feel 20
more of an individual is not necessarily to be more of an individual; there are plenty of agencies which aim to take money from working people by encouraging their feelings of individuality whilst, in fact, encouraging them to think and choose exactly like millions of others.

*Quoted in *Britain Revisited* by Tom Harrison, Gollancz, (1961).

2   You can begin to see the main physical changes by making a *25* simple tour through, for instance, one of those massive working-class districts – in the North, the Midlands or London – which are monuments to the energy and toughness of the Industrial Revolution. Most of them were established in the early and middle years of the nineteenth century. It has always surprised me that they *30* remained so little changed for so long. I was a working-class boy in the 1920s and 30s and my physical setting was substantially late-Victorian. Nonconformist chapels, battered pubs, tiny corner-shops, cheap little houses, even the uneven cobble-stones in the road, all had been there since about 1870 and framed a way of life which, in *35* many of its essentials, had not greatly changed. Look at those districts today or, if they have been cleared, go outside to the new municipal housing areas. Many of the old areas still do exist, because rehousing is slow; but the late twentieth century is emerging in a thousand details: in the wider range of goods in the corner-shop's *40* window (the shop itself may well have become a small supermarket), in the forests of television aerials, in the scatter of cars – usually second-hand –outside the doors. You can see it in people's clothes, and especially in the clothes of younger people. The clothing which identified a class, the clothing which says that you are and expect to *45* remain a worker, has almost gone. In Lancashire twenty-five years ago clogs were still often worn and the women draped black shawls round their heads and shoulders; today they can hardly be found and in their place are a variety of relatively cheap and usually attractive clothes. Some day a study will be written about the contribution of *50* one firm – Marks and Spencer's – to this change. Women's drinking cannot now be identified by the old music-hall jokes about stout and port-and-lemon. The new drinks look sophisticated, are not heavy or befuddling and are reasonably cheap. Showerings of Somerset estimated this need precisely a few years ago and produced *55* Babycham, perry (pear cider) which has been aerated and vaguely suggests champagne. Packed so as to increase this suggestion, it sells enormously. Even the fish-and-chip shops sell roast chicken and chips; and Chinese restaurants exist in towns so solidly Northern-working-class that the conjunction seems at first against nature. *60* Recreations are becoming more glossy, streamlined and centralised – bigger Bingo saloons open week after week and indoor bowling alleys on the American pattern, large and bright and electronic, are taking hold.

(*In two paragraphs here omitted the author describes changes at *65* *Leicester, for example the building of a huge car-park and plans for a civic centre.*)

3   But these are surface details, physical changes which are only pointers. The important questions have to do with the way in which habits, manners of life and attitudes, are changing under the new 70 pressures. It is easy to name the main agents of change and some have been mentioned already. Prosperity is clearly the most important. To a quick or biased observer prosperity may seem to encourage chiefly 'materialism', by which is meant the wish to have certain large consumer goods. More important, as we saw earlier, 75 prosperity can increase the sense of individual choice; and it can lengthen perspectives. It not only gives immediate opportunities but, since work is more secure, encourages a longer view, the ability to plan ahead. If you fear unemployment without warning you will not, when extra money becomes available, be likely to plough it into some 80 future project; you will be more likely to spend it at once and enjoy a brief liberation from the grind of week after week. Now working people can begin to plan ahead and, inevitably, younger people are leading the way – especially young married couples. Such an adjustment is not easy; it requires a point by point change in old outlooks, 85 old habits, old customs.

From Speaking to Each Other

1   a   The first paragraph suggests a **paradox** about individuality. Say what it is.

   b   In paragraph 1 the writer mentions some of the benefits of increased prosperity. What are some of its drawbacks?

2   a   A brief **summary** of the passage might begin:

'Hoggart suggests that working class people in the sixties felt a great sense of change in their lives. In particular, increased prosperity reduced worry and enhanced individualism.'

Continue the summary in a similar way for paragraphs 2 and 3.

   b   The writer supports his argument by various **illustrations**. Why does he mention:

'cobble-stones' *(line 34)* 'clogs' *(line 47)* Marks and Spencer's *(line 51)* Babycham *(line 56)*?

3 a The term 'working class' sometimes creates difficulties in discussion. Say why you think this is so, relating your points to the general **concept** of 'class'.

   b If Hoggart were writing a similar chapter today, what further changes in people's (i) day-to-day lives (ii) attitudes might he notice?

29 See Big Plane
Frank Smith

Frank Smith's career began in journalism but his interest in education and linguistics led him to take degrees in Australia and the USA, where he met the linguist Chomsky. He is now Professor of Education at the Ontario Institute for Studies in Education, his special field being reading. His books include *Understanding Reading* (1971), *Psycholinguistics and Reading* (1973) and *Comprehension and Learning* (1975).

1 Children who have just begun to talk often seem to make statements that are completely obvious. A child stands looking out of a window with you and says something like 'See big plane.' You may even have pointed the plane out to the child. Why then should the child bother to make the statement? The answer is because the child is learning,   *5* conducting an experiment. In fact I can imagine no fewer than three experiments being conducted at the same time in that one simple situation.

2   In the first place the child is testing the hypothesis that the object you can both clearly see in the sky *is* a plane – that it is not a bird or   *10* cloud or something else as yet unidentified. When you say 'Yes I see it' you are confirming that the object is a plane, positive feedback. Even silence is interpreted as positive feedback, since the child would expect you to make a 'correction' if the hypothesis were in error. The second hypothesis that the child might be testing concerns the   *15* sounds of the language – that the name 'plane' is the right name for the object, rather than 'pwane', 'prane' or anything else the child might say. Once again the child can assume that if you do not take the opportunity to correct then there is nothing to be corrected. A test has been successfully conducted.   *20*

3   But the third hypothesis that the child may be testing is the most interesting of all. The child may be conducting a linguistic experiment, testing whether 'See big plane' is an acceptable sentence in adult language.

4   Children do not learn to talk by imitating adults – not many   *25* adults say 'See big plane' or the other baby talk we hear from children (unless the adults are imitating children). Nor do adults give children formal lessons in how to talk. Instead children use adults as

models; children learn to talk like the adults around them by inventing their own words and rules which they modify whenever 30 they have an opportunity –through experimentation – to bring closer to adult language. One way in which children do this is by making statements in their own language for meanings which are perfectly obvious to adults and then by waiting for adults to put the statements into adult language so that they can make the 35 comparison. For example, the child at the window making the very obvious remark 'See big plane' is really asking 'Is "See big plane" a sentence in your language? Is that the way you would say it?'

5   And it is in situations like this that parents, quite unwittingly, give children the information they need to develop language for 40 themselves. The child says 'See big plane' and an adult says something like 'Yes, I can see the big plane' – the adult provides an adult surface structure for the deep structure expressed in the child's own language, a basis for comparison. If the adult says nothing, or simply continues the conversation, the child assumes the hypothesis 45 must be correct. But when adults correct – or more usually 'expand' the child's utterance into adult language – they provide children with feedback that is relevant to their hypotheses. Children do not have to ask specific questions about grammar nor do adults have to teach children specific rules of grammar –children move toward adult 50 language by conducting experiments.

6   Sometimes these experiments seem to lead children into error. Children who have been successfully making statements like 'Mummy came home' or 'Daddy went out' will suddenly start saying 'Mummy comed home' or 'Daddy goed out.' What is happening? 55 Certainly the children are not imitating adults – adults do not say 'goed' or 'comed'. Instead the children are trying out a rule which no-one has explicitly taught them but which they themselves have hypothesised. The past tense of *walk* is *walked*, the past tense of *kiss* is *kissed*, so it is a reasonable assumption that the past tense of *go* 60 should be *goed* and the past tense of *come* should be *comed*. And so children produce words like *drinked* and *eated* and *seed* that they could never possibly have heard adults say. How do they straighten all this out? Not by asking specific questions like 'Can you confirm the rule for constructing the past tense of regular verbs and give me a 65 list of exceptions?' Instead a child tests the hypothesis 'The past tense of *go* follows the regular rule' by saying 'Daddy goed.' And the parent provides the feedback by saying 'Yes – Daddy *went*.'

7   It is worthwhile to look closely at what goes on during these language-learning exchanges. The adult and the child are in effect 70 speaking different languages but because they understand each other the child can compare their different ways of saying the same thing.

122

Comprehension is at the core of the interaction, both the adult and child can make sense of what is going on. Because adults know what a child means by statements like 'See big plane' or even more 75 outlandish utterances, they can provide models of how adult language would refer to the situation, leaving the learning to the child. The situation is basically no different from that in which adults say 'There's a cat' and leave children to figure out the adult rules for recognizing cats. 80

8   The same principle of making sense of language by understanding the situation in which it is used applies in the other direction, as the child learns to *comprehend* adult speech. At the beginning of language learning infants must be able to understand sentences of a language before they can learn the language. I mean that children do 85 not come to understand utterances like: 'Would you like a drink of juice?' or even the meaning of single words like 'juice' by figuring out the language or by having someone tell them the rules. Children learn because initially they can hypothesise the meaning of a statement from the situation in which it is uttered – an adult is 90 usually carrying or pointing to a drink of juice when a sentence like 'Would you like a drink of juice?' is spoken. From such situations children can hypothesize that the next time someone mentions 'juice' the drink that they recognize as juice will be involved. The situation provides the meaning and the utterance provides the evidence – that 95 is all a child needs to construct hypotheses that can be tested on future occasions. Children do not learn language to make sense of words and sentences; they make sense of words and sentences to learn language.

9   Note here the intimate connection between comprehension and 100 learning. Just as scientists' experiments never go beyond their theories – every stage of their experiments must make sense – so children must comprehend what they are doing all the time they are learning. Everything must make sense as they test their hypotheses – 'If *drink of juice* refers to this glass of stuff in front of me, then a glass 105 of it will be around the next time *drink of juice* is mentioned.' Anything that bewilders a child will be ignored; there is nothing to be learned there. It is not nonsense that stimulates children to learn but the possibility of making sense; that is why children grow up speaking language and not imitating the noise of the air conditioner. 110

From *Reading*

123

1 **a** What three questions (paragraphs 2–3) does the child seek to answer by saying 'See big plane'?

   b What is the difference, in this context, between:

   (i) 'hypothesis' *(line 9)* and 'feedback' *(line 12)*.
   (ii) 'surface structure' and 'deep structure' *(line 43)*
   (iii) 'rule' *(lines 57, 67)* and 'model' *(line 76)*?

2 **a** A **hypothesis** may be thought of as a theory which seeks to answer a question by experiment, observation or research. The theory is then either rejected, confirmed as a general rule or modified:

Question	Hypothesis	Experiments Research Etc.	Conclusion
(i) Do sons grow taller than their mothers?	This seems to be the case.	Collect measurements of large sample of sons and mothers.	Sons grow taller than their mothers except in cases of accident or deformity.
(ii) Why are there more widows than widowers?	Because women live longer than men.	Obtain statistics for life expectancy of men and women.	In a large sample of the population there will be more widows than widowers because women have a longer mean life expectancy than men.

   Set out two other hypotheses, (iii) and (iv), in the above manner.

   b What does the child *(paragraph 6)* (i) do (ii) not do, in learning verb forms?

   c Test your own knowledge of irregular verbs by completing this chart:

Present	Perfect	Past
I drink	I have drunk	I drank
I swim	I have swum	
		I lied
I lie down		
I lay		
		I was
I go		
	I have wrought	
I do		
		I woke up

d Give three other 'outlandish' utterances *(line 76)* a young child might make, and the possible 'feedback' *(lines 12, 48, 68)* from the parent in each case.

3 a Mention one language learning problem facing:

   (i) a child deaf from birth
   (ii) a child blind from birth
   (iii) a seven-year-old moved away from his parents into a foreign language situation.

b With the writer's ideas in mind, give one argument (i) for and (ii) against adults using 'baby-talk' with their children, e.g. 'Time for beddy-byes' 'Johnny eat up din-din' 'Nice bow-wow'.

30 An Enormous Achievement
Walter Nash

Walter Nash is Senior Lecturer in English at the University of Nottingham, having previously held appointments at King's College, London, the University of Lund, Sweden, and Moray House College of Education, Edinburgh. He is the author of two books, *Our Experience of Language* (Batsford, 1971) and *Designs in Prose* (Longman, 1980), and is a regular contributor to journals and literary magazines in Britain, Europe, and the USA. His academic interests are mainly in linguistics, stylistics, and rhetoric; he is currently preparing a general guide to style and usage for writers of English. Leisure pursuits include canal-boating, painting, and music.

---

1 A man comes home from work, greets his family, goes through the motions of shrugging off the day, switches on TV, settles down to his evening meal. Presently, the screen fills with the image of the weather forecaster, who announces that a trough of low pressure is moving in over the Atlantic, that there will be rain in western Scotland before 5 late evening, reaching the north England and the Midlands by morning. The man makes a wry comment to his wife, but she is only half attentive. She is listening to the noises from next door, where a less peaceably-disposed couple are quarrelling violently, belabouring each other with a high-pitched abuse which almost disturbs the 10 composure of the mother in the house beyond, who is reading a story to her children. Across the street, an old lady is reading a letter from her son in Canada; marks on the paper make the shape of his voice. Her other son sits at the half-cleared table, speechlessly struggling with the task of completing his income-tax form. All over the city, 15 people come home, eat, talk, read, watch the evening unfold its tale of distractions or obligations. A young teacher comes back to his rented room and begins to coax on to paper a lecture, which next week he will try to read aloud as though it were a grand effusion of unpremeditated speech. Beyond his room, beyond the prattling 20 circles of the pub, beyond the newboys shouting their chalked headlines, there is the football ground, where twenty-two players and three officials provoke the cheers, catcalls, imprecations, objurgations, enthusiasm, disparagement, of twenty thousand spectators. In the small house a mile away, a man sits quite alone, 25

while in his mind a voice re-creates problems and grievances. Having no one else to talk to, he is talking to himself; for as Cicero reminds us, it is above all as talkers that we excel the beasts.

2   Imagine these, and many kindred scenes, on any evening, in any town; they represent the experience of language, as it occurs in *30* connection with the diverse experience, trivial or profound, of our lives-at-large. Our handful of examples may suggest that the experience of language is changeable and many-sided. Some of our projected characters experience language in solitude, remote from any partner in discourse other than the imagined form, the *35* whispering *alter ego*. For others, language is a shared property, a lively face-to-face exchange – or even a form of collective expression. For some, the experience of language means recognising, passively, certain ranges of symbolism; language 'happens *to*' them. There are others for whom the experience is active; they create it, it 'happens *40* *through*' them, as they themselves produce linguistic symbols. For many, language is an experience in which 'happening to' and 'happening through' follow each other in turn-and-turn-about: an ordinary conversation involves both passivity, or recognition, and activity, or production. For some, the produced or recognised *45* symbolism takes the form of speech, while for others it appears as writing. In one of our imagined instances, speech is transmitted through an especial medium (i.e. via television), one of a range of technical devices which are commonplaces of our time and which impose particular conditions on language. For some of our actors, *50* the experience of language is not associated with any strength of feeling; for others it is bound up with powerful emotions. In some cases, physical gesture and facial expression are likely to be associated significantly with the experience; in other instances, they are immaterial. *55*

3   It is clear that if we think of language as an experience, we can make a number of distinctions as to the forms this experience may take. We can also make one distinction of major importance, concerning the relevance of the experience of language to the experience of life. A review of the actors who make up our opening *60* paragraph might suggest that there are some for whom language is a relatively minor, or peripheral, element in the experience of the moment. The man in the grandstand, for instance, does not have to avail himself of the experience of language in order to have the experience of a football-match; it happens that the ability to make *65* noises adds to his pleasure, and that the shouting of slogans and directives – to say nothing of the abuse that serves to discharge violent emotions – is therefore a component of the football-watching sensation. On the other hand, for the old lady silently perusing

127

her letter, or for the children listening to their mother's reading, *70* language is much more than a component or peripheral element. It is something central, something tantamount to the experience itself – a proponent of life, if we will. For the old lady, for the children, the essentials of the moment's experience are mediated through language. Language and experience are one – the love of a son, the *75* excitement of strange events, exist by virtue of language alone; in effect, language becomes a surrogate experience. This is even true of quarrellers, who, at this imagined moment, are seen demonstrating their civilisation by fighting in phrases rather than by battling with brickbats. They are living a part of their lives at the symbolic level. *80*

4   It is an enormous achievement of mankind, to have learned to manipulate experience symbolically. We outface the beasts not merely because we speak, but because by speaking we make things happen, or even make happenings without things. We make words lever our world, in doing so we manifest the fact that our language *85* and the social environment (or environments) in which it is exercised are governed by conventions of usage which we all recognise, and on which we rely as prerequisites to communication and to the continuity of our experience. We take a great deal for granted about the world we are brought up in, and about the conventions of *90* symbolism which give us our guidance and purchase in that world. If, for example, I take a bus-ride, and ask the conductor for a 'sevenpenny, please', I expect my words to produce a certain effect. They initiate on the conductor's part an action, the central and significant element in which is the handing to me of a small piece of *95* paper called a ticket. The handing over of the ticket and my continued possession of it during the time that I am on the bus, are socially important. I waste no time in offering my sevenpence to anybody and everybody on the vehicle. I keep it for the person whose special dress and equipment mark him out as the official called the *100* conductor; and it is to him that I speak the words that begin the ritual of ticket-issuing. I know what to do and what to say and what will happen, because I have long since learned the conventions of language and situation that pertain in my society. If the conventions were to change every day, if tomorrow it should become necessary to *105* say 'three and a half rapid haddocks', upon which the conductor would hand over a plastic rose, and if the day after tomorrow the form were to be 'an eggcupful' and the response the marking of my forehead with coloured chalk – then obviously life would become unendurably various, and I could rely on nothing, learn nothing, *110* assume nothing, do nothing of any importance, because of the unpredictability of commonplace situations. But situations, on the whole, are not unpredictable, and the conventions of language and

behaviour do not change so violently and absurdly.

5   Perhaps this is all too obvious; but it cannot be said too *115*
emphatically or too often that language depends, for its working
power, on the existence of two conventions, the one social or
environmental, the other having to do with the symbolism and
structure of language itself. It is sometimes hard for people not
trained to the study of language to accept fully the principle that the *120*
symbols of language are conventional, and that the conventions are
at bottom quite arbitrary. We do not use a particular set of vowels
(for example) because they are proper to right-thinking people, or a
certain tense-system because it embodies the robustness of the
national character. Of course it would be absurd to suppose that *125*
language is like that; and of course there should be no need to say
(but there always is) that it is not an immutable ordinance of heaven.
Englishmen order their affairs with the help of a symbolic system
which is neither superior nor inferior to, but merely different from,
the one used by Frenchmen. It is also different from the system used *130*
by Englishmen living a thousand years ago. Symbolic systems vary,
and change. At the moment, we accept a certain system as a matter of
convention, and put it into daily operation as a *code*. The image of
our activity in language as a process of encoding and decoding
signals may be a little too machine-like, and may especially repel *135*
those who look to language for the stuff of poetry, for the medium of
all that is startling and sweet in human thought. Let us insist,
therefore, that the word *code* is simply a useful metaphor. Its
implication of a design in the production of words need cast no
coldness on our desire for the Word.   *140*

From *Our Experience of Language*

---

1   Complete this **summary** of the passage by putting in each space a
     word from the following list:

The author begins with a cluster of _____ of language in   a)
_____ use.   b)
    The second paragraph analyses the examples into vari-
ous _____ of language experience: – solitary or _____; c) d)
passive or _____; speech (sometimes electronically   e)
transmitted) or _____; emotional or non-emotional; and   f)
language accompanied by _____ or independent of it.   g)

129

In paragraph 3 a _____ is made between language   h)
which is _____ and that which is central and almost a part   i)
of _____ itself.   j)

The fourth paragraph deals with the _____ nature of   k)
language and its _____ to affect our _____ through l) m)
general agreement on usage. By this agreement we all know
what _____ or _____ words stand for, and we have n) o)
confidence that the _____ of language will not suddenly   p)
change.

Finally, the author reiterates the _____ of convention-   q)
ality (i.e. social acceptance of the meanings of language)
and symbolism (i.e. an agreed but _____ correspondence   r)
between language and the world). Though all language
systems are symbolic, they differ and they _____. Our   s)
daily use of language can be thought of as a kind of _____   t)
and decoding.

symbolic	actions	gesture	environment
categories	distinction	encoding	arbitrary
evolve	experience	examples	active
writing	concepts	everyday	objects
conventions	peripheral	power	shared

2 a The author sometimes leaves the reader to fill out a point from
his own experience. How would you do this for:

   (i) 'shrugging off the day' *(line 2)*
  (ii) 'a wry comment' *(line 7)*
 (iii) 'a less peaceably disposed couple' *(lines 8–9)*
 (iv) 'make the shape of his voice' *(line 13)*
  (v) 'distractions or obligations' *(line 17)*
 (vi) 'coax' *(line 18)*
 (vii) 'the whispering *alter ego*' *(lines 35–36)*
(viii) 'battling with brickbats' *(lines 79–80)*
 (ix) 'the system used by Englishman living a thousand years
      ago' *(lines 130–131)*
  (x) 'our desire for the Word' *(line 140)?*

b (i) Students of language have made counts of the **frequency**
of words in English (e.g. Thorndike and Large: *The
Teacher's Word Book of 30,000 Words*, 1944, and West: *A
General Service List*, 1953).

Arrange these words from the passage in an estimated order
of frequency, with the commonest first:

'task' *(line 15)* 'room' *(line 18)* 'objurgations' *(line 24)* 'kindred' *(line 29)* 'television' *(line 48)* 'any' *(line 51)* 'mother' *(line 70)* 'surrogate' *(line 77)* 'environment' *(line 86)* 'immutable' *(line 127)*.

(ii) Add five other words from the passage which might come in the latter part of the range.

(iii) Look up the meanings of all the unfamiliar words in the list, decide which words would be useful additions to your vocabulary and say how you would learn them.

c   The passage contains both **abstract concepts**, e.g.
'the experience of language is changeable and many-sided' *(lines 32–33)*
'It is an enormous achievement of mankind to have learned to manipulate experience symbolically' *(lines 81–82)*
and **concrete examples**, e.g.
'the handing to me of a small piece of paper called a ticket' *(lines 95–96)*
'an eggcupful' *(line 108)*.

(i) Find two more of each.

(ii) Suggest four other examples the author might have used in paragraph 1.

(iii) Formulate an abstract concept on the theme of Justice *or* Suffering *or* The Purpose of Life.

3 a   Walter Nash continues his chapter by dealing with such features of language as Sound, the Graphic System, Grammar and the Lexicon.

(i) Under which of these headings would you place these statements by the author:
   A 'Looking at the make-up and function of words, phrases and clauses, as revealed through their operation in English sentences, must be a major part of the task. . . '
   B 'The Eskimo languages have a number of different words for snow.'
   C 'A good deal of information in language is carried by the progressive variations of pitch and accent which we call intonation patterns.'
   D 'If the letters are badly formed, then more and more of the total substance of writing has to be scrutinised in order to interpret the message fully.'

(ii) Say which of A to D above are **generalisations** and which **examples**.

131

b The 'unpredictability of commonplace situations' *(line 112)* is often part of the scene in Lewis Carroll's *Alice* books.

Describe an incident in a world where conventions of language and behaviour change unexpectedly.

31 Incidental Gestures
Desmond Morris

Desmond Morris is a professional zoologist and a Fellow of Wolfson College, Oxford where his research field is animal behaviour. He was Curator of Mammals at the London Zoo, 1959–67. His publications include *The Mammals* (1965) and, with Ramona Morris, *Men and Snakes, Men and Apes* and *Men and Pandas* (1965–66). He is probably best known for *The Naked Ape* (1967), *The Human Zoo* (1969) and *Intimate Behaviour* (1971) in which he explores the implications of viewing man as a biological species. *Manwatching* explores human 'body language' in all its variety.

1 Many of our actions are basically non-social, having to do with problems of personal body care, body comfort and body transportation; we clean and groom ourselves with a variety of scratchings, rubbings and wipings; we cough, yawn and stretch our limbs; we eat and drink; we prop ourselves up in restful postures, folding our arms 5 and crossing our legs; we sit, stand, squat and recline, in a whole range of different positions; we crawl, walk and run in varying gaits and styles. But although we do these things for our own benefit, we are not always unaccompanied when we do them. Our companions learn a great deal about us from these 'personal' actions – not merely 10 that we are scratching because we itch or that we are running because we are late, but also, from the way we do them, what kind of personalities we possess and what mood we are in at the time.

2   Sometimes the mood-signal transmitted unwittingly in this way is one that we would rather conceal, if we stopped to think about it. 15 Occasionally we do become self-consciously aware of the 'mood broadcasts' and 'personality displays' we are making and we may then try to check ourselves. But often we do not, and the message goes out loud and clear.

3   For instance, if a student props his head on his hands while 20 listening to a boring lecture, his head-on-hands action operates both mechanically and gesturally. As a mechanical act, it is simply a case of supporting a tired head – a physical act that concerns no one but the student himself. At the same time, though, it cannot help operating as a gestural act, beaming out a visual signal to his 25 companions, and perhaps to the lecturer himself, telling them that he is bored.

4   In such a case his gesture was not deliberate and he may not even have been aware that he was transmitting it. If challenged, he would claim that he was not bored at all, but merely tired. If he were *30* honest –or impolite – he would have to admit that excited attention easily banishes tiredness, and that a really fascinating speaker need never fear to see a slumped, headpropped figure like his in the audience.

5   In the schoolroom, the teacher who barks at his pupils to 'sit up *35* straight' is demanding, by right, the attention-posture that he should have gained by generating interest in his lesson. It says a great deal for the power of gesture-signals that he feels more 'attended-to' when he sees his pupils sitting up straight, even though he is consciously well aware of the fact that they have just been forcibly un-slumped, *40* rather than genuinely excited by his teaching.

6   Many of our Incidental Gestures provide mood information of a kind that neither we *nor our companions* become consciously alerted to. It is as if there is an underground communication system operating just below the surface of our social encounters. We *45* perform an act and it is observed. Its meaning is read, but not out loud. We 'feel' the mood, rather than analyse it. Occasionally an action of this type becomes so characteristic of a particular situation that we do eventually identify it – as when we say of a difficult problem: 'That will make him scratch his head', indicating that we *50* do understand the link that exists between puzzlement and the Incidental Gesture of head-scratching. But frequently this type of link operates below the conscious level, or is missed altogether.

7   Where the links are clearer, we can, of course, manipulate the situation and use our Incidental Gestures in a contrived way. If a *55* student listening to a lecture is not tired, but wishes to insult the speaker, he can deliberately adopt a bored, slumped posture, knowing that its message will get across. This is a Stylised Incidental Gesture –a mechanical action that is being artificially employed as a pure signal. Many of the common 'courtesies' also fall into this *60* category –as when we greedily eat up a plate of food that we do not want and which we do not like, merely to transmit a suitably grateful signal to our hosts. Controlling our Incidental Gestures in this way is one of the processes that every child must learn as it grows up and learns to adapt to the rules of conduct of the society in which it lives. *65*

From *Manwatching*, 1977

1 a How would you decide whether an action is social or 'non-social'? *(line 1)*

b (i) Morris divides non-social actions into three **categories**. *(lines 1–8)*
    Complete this chart to show the categories and **examples** of each:

Non-social actions		
1.	2. Body comfort	3. . . . .
cleaning	coughing	. . . .
grooming	yawning	etc.
. . . .	. . . .	
etc.	etc.	

   (ii) From your own observation give two examples of each type.

c Describe two contrasting people, A and B, and show how (i) their personalities and (ii) their moods might be reflected by their incidental gestures.

2 a Find in paragraph 2 the **generalisation** supported by the example in paragraph 3.

b The author often emphasises his points by placing one word or phrase in **opposition** to another. What word or phrase in paragraph 2 is opposed to 'unwittingly' *(line 14)*; in paragraph 3 to 'a physical act that concerns no one but the student himself' *(lines 23–24)*; and in paragraph 5 to 'forcibly un-slumped' *(line 40)*?

c Explain the opposition between an Incidental Gesture and a Stylised Incidental Gesture *(paragraph 7)*.

3 a In a paragraph prior to this extract Morris distinguishes Primary Gestures (like waving, winking and pointing) from Incidental Gestures. Describe a domestic crisis in the life of Pat Perry (male or female) including at least six gestures of both types.

b Actors often rely on gesture to communicate feeling. Mention two states of feeling that would be particularly difficult to convey in this way.

32 Summerhill Education Vs Standard Education

A. S. Neill

A. S. Neill (1883–1976) was born and educated in Scotland and read English at Edinburgh University. He taught in Britain and helped found an international school in Dresden. He was interested in the work of modern psychologists such as Freud and Reich and put some of their ideas into practice in his school Summerhill at Leiston, Suffolk. The school, one of the earliest 'progressive' or 'free discipline' schools, aroused much discussion in educational circles. Neill's books on bringing up children include: *The Problem Child* (1926), *The Problem Parent* (1932), *The Problem Teacher* (1939), *Hearts not Heads* (1945), *The Problem Family* (1948) and *Talking of Summerhill* (1967).

1 I hold that the aim of life is to find happiness, which means to find interest. Education should be a preparation for life. Our culture has not been very successful. Our education, politics, and economics lead to war. Our medicines have not done away with disease. Our religion has not abolished usury and robbery. Our boasted humani- 5 tarianism still allows public opinion to approve of the barbaric sport of hunting. The advances of the age are advances in mechanism – in radio and television, in electronics, in jet planes. New world wars threaten, for the world's social conscience is still primitive.

2 If we feel like questioning today, we can pose a few awkward 10 questions. Why does man seem to have many more diseases than animals have? Why does man hate and kill in war when animals do not? Why does cancer increase? Why are there so many suicides? So many insane sex crimes? Why the hate that is anti-Semitism? Why Negro hating and lynching? Why backbiting and spite? Why is sex 15 obscene and a leering joke? Why is being a bastard a social disgrace? Why the continuance of religions that have long ago lost their love and hope and charity? Why, a thousand whys about our vaunted state of civilised eminence!

3 I ask these questions because I am by profession a teacher, one 20 who deals with the young. I ask these questions because those so often asked by teachers are the unimportant ones, the ones about school subjects. I ask what earthly good can come out of discussions

about French or ancient history or what not when these subjects don't matter a jot compared to the larger question of life's natural *25* fulfilment – of man's inner happiness.

4   How much of our education is real doing, real self-expression? Handwork is too often the making of a pin tray under the eye of an expert. Even the Montessori system, well-known as a system of directed play, is an artificial way of making the child learn by doing. *30* It has nothing creative about it.

5   In the home, the child is always being taught. In almost every home, there is always at least one un-grownup grownup who rushes to show Tommy how his new engine works. There is always someone to lift the baby up on a chair when baby wants to examine something *35* on the wall. Every time we show Tommy how his engine works we are stealing from that child the joy of life – the joy of discovery – the joy of overcoming an obstacle. Worse! We make that child come to believe that he is inferior, and must depend on help.

6   Parents are slow in realising how unimportant the learning side of *40* school is. Children, like adults, learn what they want to learn. All prize-giving and marks and exams sidetrack proper personality development. Only pedants claim that learning from books is education.

7   Books are the least important apparatus in a school. All that any *45* child needs is the three R's; the rest should be tools and clay and sports and theatre and paint and freedom.

8   Most of the school work that adolescents do is simply a waste of time, of energy, of patience. It robs youth of its right to play and play and play; it puts old heads on young shoulders. *50*

9   When I lecture to students at teacher training colleges and universities, I am often shocked at the un-grownupness of these lads and lasses stuffed with useless knowledge. They know a lot; they shine in dialectics; they can quote the classics – but in their outlook on life many of them are infants. For they have been taught *to know*, *55* but have not been allowed *to feel*. These students are friendly, pleasant, eager, but something is lacking – the emotional factor, the power to subordinate thinking to feeling. I talk to these of a world they have missed and go on missing. Their textbooks do not deal with human character, or with love, or with freedom, or with self- *60* determination. And so the system goes on, aiming only at standards of book learning – goes on separating the head from the heart.

10   It is time that we were challenging the school's notion of work. It is taken for granted that every child should learn mathematics, history, geography, some science, a little art, and certainly literature. It is *65* time we realised that the average young child is not much interested in any of these subjects.

137

11   I prove this with every new pupil. When told that the school is free, every new pupil cries, 'Hurrah! You won't catch me doing dull arithmetic and things!' 70

12   I am not decrying learning. But learning should come after play. And learning should not be deliberately seasoned with play to make it palatable.

13   Learning is important – but not to everyone. Nijinsky could not pass his school exams in St Petersburg, and he could not enter the 75 State Ballet without passing those exams. He simply could not learn school subjects – his mind was elsewhere. They faked an exam for him, giving him the answers with the papers – so a biography says. What a loss to the world if Nijinsky had had really to pass those exams! 80

14   Creators learn what they want to learn in order to have the tools that their originality and genius demand. We do not know how much creation is killed in the classroom with its emphasis on learning.

15   I have seen a girl weep nightly over her geometry. Her mother wanted her to go to the university, but the girl's whole soul was 85 artistic. I was delighted when I heard that she had failed her college entrance exams for the seventh time. Possibly, the mother would now allow her to go on the stage as she longed to do.

16   Some time ago, I met a girl of fourteen in Copenhagen who had spent three years in Summerhill and had spoken perfect English here. 90 'I suppose you are at the top of your class in English,' I said.

17   She grimaced ruefully. 'No, I'm at the bottom of my class, because I don't know English grammar,' she said. I think that disclosure is about the best commentary on what adults consider education.

18   Indifferent scholars who, under discipline, scrape through college 95 or university and become unimaginative teachers, mediocre doctors, and incompetent lawyers would possibly be good mechanics or excellent bricklayers or first-rate policemen.

19   We have found that the boy who cannot or will not learn to read until he is, say, fifteen is always a boy with a mechanical bent who 100 later on becomes a good engineer or electrician. I should not dare dogmatise about girls who never go to lessons, especially to mathematics and physics. Often such girls spend much time with needlework, and some, later on in life, take up dressmaking and designing. It is an absurd curriculum that makes a prospective 105 dressmaker study quadratic equations or Boyle's Law.

20   Caldwell Cook wrote a book called *The Play Way*, in which he told how he taught English by means of play. It was a fascinating book, full of good things, yet I think it was only a new way of bolstering the theory that learning is of the utmost importance. 110 Cook held that learning was so important that the pill should be

sugared with play. This notion that unless a child is learning something the child is wasting his time is nothing less than a curse – a curse that blinds thousands of teachers and most school inspectors. Fifty years ago the watchword was 'Learn through doing.' Today *115* the watchword is 'Learn through playing.' Play is thus used only as a means to an end, but to what good end I do not really know.

21   If a teacher sees children playing with mud, and he thereupon improves the shining moment by holding forth about river-bank erosion, what end has he in view? What child cares about river *120* erosion? Many so-called educators believe that it does not matter what a child learns as long as he is *taught* something. And, of course, with schools as they are – just mass-production factories – what can a teacher do but teach something and come to believe that teaching, in itself, matters most of all? *125*

22   When I lecture to a group of teachers, I commence by saying that I am not going to speak about school subjects or discipline or classes. For an hour my audience listens in rapt silence; and after the sincere applause, the chairman announces that I am ready to answer questions. At least three-quarters of the questions deal with subjects *130* and teaching.

23   I do not tell this in any superior way. I tell it sadly to show how the classroom walls and the prisonlike buildings narrow the teacher's outlook, and prevent him from seeing the true essentials of education. His work deals with the part of a child that is above the *135* neck; and perforce, the emotional, vital part of the child is foreign territory to him.

24   I wish I could see a bigger movement of rebellion among our younger teachers. Higher education and university degrees do not make a scrap of difference in confronting the evils of society. A *140* learned neurotic is not any different than an unlearned neurotic.

25   In all countries, capitalist, socialist, or communist, elaborate schools are built to educate the young. But all the wonderful labs and workshops do nothing to help John or Peter or Ivan surmount the emotional damage and the social evils bred by the pressure on him *145* from his parents, his schoolteachers, and the pressure of the coercive quality of our civilisation.

From *Summerhill*

139

1 a 'Just mass-production factories' is A. S. Neill's opinion of 'schools as they are' *(line 123)*.

  (i) What does he mean?
  (ii) Do you agree with him?

b Neill makes a number of provocative **assertions**, e.g.
'Books are the least important apparatus in a school' *(line 45);* 'Most of the school work that adolescents do is simply a waste of time, of energy, of patience' *(lines 48–49)*.

Find two more such assertions and say whether and why you agree, partly agree or disagree in each case.

c Why might some women object to paragraph 19?

2 a The author's argument is partly based on **opposition** (or **antithesis**). Thus in paragraph 3 he opposes 'school subjects' to 'life's natural fulfilment'; in paragraph 4, 'real doing, real self-expression' and 'creative' to 'directed play' and 'an artificial way'. Point out one or more antitheses in each of the paragraphs 6, 7, 8, 9, 12 and 14.

b Several **examples** are given by the author. What point is he illustrating by:

  (i) the grownup who rushes to show Tommy how his new engine works *(lines 33–34)*
  (ii) the new pupil who cries 'Hurrah!' *(line 69)*
  (iii) Nijinsky *(paragraph 13)*
  (iv) the girl weeping over her geometry *(paragraph 15)*
  (v) the girl in Copenhagen *(paragraphs 16 and 17)*
  (vi) the children playing with mud *(paragraph 21)*?

c Education is an important **concept** in all societies. Two books dealing with important present-day words and ideas are Raymond Williams' *Keywords* and *The Fontana Dictionary of Modern Thought*, edited by A. Bullock and O. Stallybrass.

  (i) which of these words from the passage would you expect to appear in one or both of the books:

  (from paragraph 1) 'culture', 'politics', 'usury', 'hunting' (from paragraph 2) 'diseases', 'backbiting', 'religion', 'eminence' (from paragraph 9) 'un-grownupness', 'dialectics', 'character', 'self-determination'?

(ii) Justify your choice of one word and your rejection of one.

(iii) From paragraphs 24 and 25 choose five words you would expect to find in the books mentioned.

(iv) Justify your choice of two of them.

3 Neill's book gives many other details about his school, Summerhill, e.g.

a 'Lessons are optional. Children can go to them or stay away from them – for years if they want to. There *is* a timetable – but only for the teachers.' *(page 20)* freedom to Learn

b 'When Billy, aged five, told me to get out of his birthday party because I hadn't been invited, I went at once without hesitation – just as Billy gets our of my room when I don't want his company.' *(page 24)*

c 'Sometimes a case of stealing is brought up at the General School Meeting. There is never any punishment for stealing, but there is always reparation. Often children will come to me and say, "John stole some coins from David. Is this a case for psychology, or shall we bring it up?"' *(page 56)*

(i) What point about education do you think Neill is making in each case?

(ii) Imagine that a regular General Meeting has recently been instituted in a school known to you. Describe the discussion of two items and the decision made in each case.

33 Scripts People Live
Claude M. Steiner

Claude Steiner is an American clinical psychologist who worked closely with Eric Berne. The latter's book, *Games People Play* (1964), became widely known as an exposition of 'transactional analysis' psychological theory. *Scripts People Live*, in which the Berne approach is discussed and exemplified, grew out of *Games Alcoholics Play* (1971). According to the publisher, its message is 'It's not too late to decide what kind of script you want for your life – if any at all.' Hogie Wyckoff has similar professional interests. She contributed a number of 'scripts' to *Scripts People Live*, including 'Creeping Beauty'.

A THE SIGNIFICANCE OF SCRIPT ANALYSIS IN PSYCHIATRY

1 When people find that their lives have become unmanageable, filled with unhappiness and emotional pain, they have been known to turn to psychiatry for an answer. Psychiatry, however, is not the principal form of counsel that is sought by most people—who generally tend to go to ministers, physicians, and friends before they resort to the 5 use of psychiatric help. Most Americans distrust psychiatry and resort to psychiatric counsel only when too desperate to be able to avoid it any longer or when they encounter a psychiatric approach which they can relate to and appreciate.

2   Mental health associations around the country are busy convinc- 10 ing people that they should make use of psychiatric services. Yet, most people avoid them, and when in emotional difficulty make do without any help, letting nature takes its curative course. The fact that people in emotional difficulties do not consult psychiatrists is seen by psychiatrists to be due to lack of judgment and is even 15 interpreted by some to be the result of their will to 'fall (and remain) ill.' In my mind, people have, so far, shown good judgment in their rejection of the psychiatric help that is available to most.

3   Of the few who do consult psychiatrists, most (in my opinion) are not harmed. On the other hand, U.S. Senator Tom Eagleton's short- 20 lived bid for the Vice-Presidential office of the United States in the 1972 elections illustrates how harmful psychiatry can be. As Ronald Laing has pointed out, Eagleton committed the error of consulting a

psychiatrist who with his diagnosis and treatment (electro-shock therapy) marked him and defeated him for any major future political *25* aspirations. He could have chosen a psychiatrist like Eric Berne, who didn't use shock therapy and who would have helped him over his depression with other means.

4   Most persons who consult psychiatrists are basically 'cooled out,' pacified, brought back into temporary functioning; and a few are *30* genuinely helped. I believe that psychiatrists who succeed in helping their clients do so because they reject the bulk of their psychiatric training and adopt a stance which comes out of their own experiences, personal wisdom, and humanistic convictions which overpower the oppressive and harmful teachings of psychiatric *35* training.

5   Psychiatry is taught in what appears to be several different 'schools of thought' with different points of view. But in my mind the minor disagreements between the different schools of psychiatric thought are negligible; actually these minor differences only serve to *40* obscure the fact that, fundamentally, psychiatric theories agree on three main points:

1. Some people are normal, and some people are abnormal. The line of demarcation is sharp, and psychiatrists act as if they can distinguish between those who are not disturbed and those who are *45* disturbed or 'mentally ill'.

2. The reason for 'mental illness' and emotional disturbance is to be found within people, and psychiatric practice consists of diagnosing the illness and working with the individual to cure it. Some of the disturbances are incurable, such as alcoholism, schizophrenia or *50* manic-depressive psychosis. Psychiatry's job is to make the 'victims' of such 'illness' comfortable in their misery, teaching them to adapt and cope, often with the use of drugs.

3. Persons who are mentally ill have no understanding of their illness, and very little if any control over it, just as is supposedly the case with *55* physical diseases.

6   These three assumptions permeate psychiatric training and are deeply embedded in the minds of the majority (more than 50%) of those who practice psychotherapy whether they be (in descending order of prestige) physicians, psychologists, social workers, nurses, *60* probation officers or any other trained psychotherapist.

7   It is little wonder that most people who get into emotional difficulties are loath to consult a psychotherapist. We do not want to hear that the trouble is to be found entirely within us and that, at the same time, we have no control or understanding of our difficulties. *65*

We do not want to hear these things about ourselves not because we are 'resistant to change' or 'motivated' for psychotherapy, but because they are not true, because they insult our intelligence, and because they rob us of our power to control our lives and destinies.

8   Script theory offers an alternative to this thinking. First of all, we *70* believe that people are born OK, that when they get into emotional difficulties they still remain OK, and that their difficulties can be understood and solved by examining their interactions with other human beings, and by understanding the oppressive injunctions and attributions laid on them in childhood and maintained throughout *75* life. Transactional script analysis offers an approach, not in the form of mystified theories understandable only to psychotherapists, but in the form of explanations which are commonsensical and understandable to the person who needs them, namely, the person in emotional difficulties.   *80*

9   Script analysis can be called a decision theory rather than a disease theory of emotional disturbance. Script theory is based on the belief that people make conscious life plans in childhood or early adolescence which influence and make predictable the rest of their lives. Persons whose lives are based on such decisions are said to have *85* scripts. Like diseases, scripts have an onset, a course, and an outcome. Because of this similarity, life scripts are easily mistaken for diseases. However, because scripts are based on consciously willed decisions rather than on morbid tissue changes, they can be revoked or undecided by similarly willed decisions. Tragic life scripts *90* such as suicide, drug addiction, or 'incurable mental illnesses' such as 'schizophrenia' or 'manic-depressive psychosis,' are the result of scripting rather than disease. Because these disturbances are scripts rather than incurable diseases it is possible to develop an understanding and approach which enables competent therapists to help *95* their clients to, as Berne said, 'close down the show and put a new one on the road.' Questioning the negative assumptions of psychiatry also generates positive expectance and hope, whose importance Frank and Goldstein have amply documented. From their studies it is clear that the assumptions of mental health workers *100* about their clients have an extremely strong influence on the outcome of their work. Their research shows that when there exists an assumption of illness and chronicity on the part of the workers the effect is that of producing chronicity and illness in the clients, while an assumption of curability on the part of the worker will be *105* associated with an improvement on the part of the client. Thus, considering emotional disturbance as some form of illness, as many who work with people do, is potentially harmful and may in fact be promoting illness in people who seek help from psychiatrists. On the

other hand, the assumption that psychiatric disturbances are curable *110* since they are based on reversible decisions frees in people their potent, innate tendencies to recover and overthrow their unhappiness. Workers who offer positive expectancy, coupled with problem-solving expertise, make it possible for people in emotional difficulties to take power over their lives and produce their own new, *115* satisfying life plans.

10   The following pages describe life scripts, and how to work with them, using transactional analysis . . .

B   CREEPING BEAUTY

11 *Life Course:* She has the standard attributes of so-called 'media beauty', but she doesn't feel very good about herself as a person and *120* really doesn't believe she is lovely. Rather, she thinks of herself as being shallow and ugly underneath the veneer. When she looks into the mirror she doesn't see her beauty but only sees her blemishes and imperfections. This is called the 'Beautiful Woman Syndrome' which paradoxically frequently occurs with women who do not see their *125* own beauty because they focus on individual parts of their appearance which may not be attractive when seen separately. She sees herself as deceiving everyone who thinks she is beautiful and thinks they're fools for buying the deception. She gets too many strokes for being beautiful and discounts them all. She wants to be *130* liked as a person, but no one is willing to see past her exterior beauty. Any man with her gets strokes for having such a lovely possession on his arm. She is constantly in search of a Prince Charming who will end all her troubles by making her truly beautiful and valuable with his pure love. She is angry that people don't appreciate her primarily *135* as a human being and tends to fight back by chain-smoking and presenting a very sloppy appearance around intimate friends. She gets men to come across with as much as they will and then doesn't deliver the goods (herself). She primarily experiences herself as a Victim. Too often other women see her as a crafty competitor for *140* men's attention and envy her beauty. Because of her good looks she often gets what she wants very easily. This special treatment makes it unnecessary for her to learn to cooperate with people so she can be a bit of a prima donna at times.

12   Because she doesn't use her Adult in her relationship with Prince *145* Charming, he eventually 'rips her off' emotionally. Later, when she loses her media beauty, she continues the same hostile behavior toward others that she has always manifested, only now people think she is just being a 'bitch' for no reason. Too often she ends up alone, loving no one, not even herself.   *150*

13 *Counterscript:* It appears that her life is wonderfully happy when she is head-over-heels in love with her Prince Charming. It looks great for about six months and then slowly begins to tarnish when he gets interested in a new beautiful woman.

14 *Injunctions and Attributions:*   *155*
Your beauty is only skin deep
Don't be close to people
Don't be you

15 *Decision:* People seem to respond to her only as a pretty face and not as a person, so she decides since she seems to be incapable of being *160* treated and respected as an effective social agent to sell herself as a sex object in order to get some of what she wants.

16 *Mythical Heroine:* She has a morbid fascination with the Marilyn Monroe legend, and admires prominent movie and television stars.

17 *Somatic Component:* Her body is very beautiful, but she has little *165* feeling in it. . . . When she smiles only her mouth moves so as not to wrinkle up her eyes.

18 *Games:*
Rapo   *170*
If it Weren't For You
Blemish (on herself)

19 *Therapist's Role in the Script:* He becomes sexually aroused by her and propositions her so she can then discount anything he might *175* have to say.

20 *Antithesis:* She starts demanding strokes for the qualities people like in her other than her beauty and she refuses to accept strokes just for her physical presence. She begins to like herself as she is, stops playing 'Blemish' on herself, and begins to thoroughly enjoy her true inner and outer beauty. She starts to do things that are meaningful to *180* her and works in a women's group to learn how to cooperate to get what she wants.

21   She decides to use her Adult to build a cooperative relationship with a man who appreciates her as a person. She starts enjoying her power while creating her life the way she wants it to be and *185* appreciates what she has to work with in herself.

from *Scripts People Live*

1 a What is the difference between psychiatry and psychology?

b What might 'ministers, physicians and friends' *(line 5)* have in common with psychiatrists?

2 a In paragraphs 3–7 the author criticises some aspects of psychiatry.

(i) Give one criticism from each paragraph.
(ii) Of all the criticisms made by the author say which you think are the most serious. Give reasons.

b In paragraphs 8–9 the author suggests that 'script theory' and 'script analysis' have advantages over traditional psychiatry. Mention two of the advantages claimed.

c What evidence is there, in the case of your own life, that you (i) are (ii) are not living a 'script' you have chosen?

3 a 'Creeping Beauty' is one of the many 'life scripts' analysed in the book from which the extract is taken. By research and discussion establish the meaning of

(i) the sub-headings (*Life Course, Counterscript* etc.) in paragraphs 11–20
(ii) these technical terms:
'syndrome' *(line 124)* 'strokes' *(lines 130, 132, 176)* 'use her Adult' *(line 183)*.

b Write a page from a novel about a 'Creeping Beauty'.

34 The Trouble With People

Vance Packard

Vance Packard has worked for *The American Magazine, Colliers* and many other journals, as well as producing a series of books whose titles speak for themselves: *The Status Seekers* (1959); *The Waste Makers* (1960); *The Pyramid Climbers* (1962); *The Naked Society* (1964); *The Sexual Wilderness* (1968); *A Nation of Strangers* (1972) and *The People Shapers* (1977).

===========

In very few instances do people really know what they want, even when they say they do. ('Advertising Age')

1 The trend in marketing to the depth approach was largely impelled by difficulties the marketers kept encountering in trying to persuade people to buy all the products their companies could fabricate.

2   One particularly disturbing difficulty was the apparent perversity and unpredictability of the prospective customers. Marketers re- 5 peatedly suffered grievous losses in campaigns that by all the rules of logic should have succeeded. The marketers felt increasing dissatisfaction with their conventional methods for sizing up a market. These methods were known in the trade most commonly as 'nose-counting'. Under nose-counting, statistic-minded interviewers 10 would determine the percentage of married women, ages twenty-one to thirty-five, in Omaha, Nebraska, who said they wanted, and would buy, a three-legged stove if it cost no more than $249.

3   The trouble with this approach, they found, was that what people might tell interviewers had only a remote bearing on how the people 15 would actually behave in a buying situation when confronted with a three-legged stove or almost anything else.

4   Gradually many perceptive marketers began becoming suspicious of three basic assumptions they had made, in their efforts to be logical, concerning the predictable behaviour of human beings, 20 especially customers.

5   First, they decided, you can't assume that people know what they want.

6   A major ketchup maker kept getting complaints about its bottle, so it made a survey. Most of the people interviewed said they would 25 prefer another type the company was considering. When the

company went to the expense of bringing out this other bottle in test markets, it was overwhelmingly rejected in favour of the old bottle, even by people who had favoured it in interviews. In a survey of male beer drinkers the men expressed a strong preference for a 'nice dry 30 beer'. When they were then asked how a beer could be dry they were stumped. Those who were able to offer any answers at all revealed widely different notions.

7   Second, some marketers concluded, you can't assume people will tell you the truth about their wants and dislikes even if they know 35 them. What you are more likely to get, they decided, are answers that will protect the informants in their steadfast endeavour to appear to the world as really sensible, intelligent rational beings. One management consulting firm has concluded that accepting the word of a customer as to what he wants is 'the least reliable index the 40 manufacturer can have on what he ought to do to win customers'.

8   The Advertising Research Foundation took magazines to task for asking people what magazines they read frequently, and naively accepting the answers given as valid. The people, it contended, are likely to admit reading only magazines of high prestige value. One 45 investigator suggests that if you seriously accepted people's answers you might assume that *Atlantic Monthly* is America's most-read magazine and some of the confession magazines the least read; whereas actually the confession magazines in question may have twice times the readership of *Atlantic Monthly*. 50

9   A brewery making two kinds of beer made a survey to find what kind of people drank each beer, as a guide to its merchandisers. It asked people known to favour its general brand name: 'Do you drink the light or the regular?' To its astonishment it found people reporting they drank light over the regular by better than three to 55 one. The truth of the matter was that for years the company, to meet consumer demand, had been brewing nine times as much regular beer as light beer. It decided that in asking people that question it was in effect asking: Do you drink the kind preferred by people of refinement and discriminating taste, or do you just drink the regular 60 stuff?

10   The Color Research Institute conducted an experiment after it began suspecting the reliability of people's comments. Women while waiting for a lecture had the choice of two waiting rooms. One was a functional modern chamber with gentle tones. It had been carefully 65 designed for eye ease and to promote a relaxed feeling. The other room was a traditional room filled with period furniture, oriental rugs, expensive-looking wallpaper.

11   It was found that virtually all the women instinctively went into the Swedish modern room to do their waiting. Only when every chair 70

was filled did the women start to overflow into the more ornate room. After the lecture the ladies were asked, 'Which of those two rooms do you like the better?' They looked thoughtfully at the two rooms, and then eighty-four per cent of them said the period room was the nicer room. *75*

12   In another case the institute asked a group of people if they borrowed money from personal-loan companies. Every person said no. Some of them virtually shouted their answer. The truth was that all those selected for interviewing were people who were listed in the records of a local loan company as borrowers. *80*

13   Psychologists at the McCann-Erickson advertising agency asked a sampling of people why they didn't buy one client's product – kippered herring. The main reason the people gave under direct questioning was that they just didn't like the taste of kippers. More persistent probing however uncovered the fact that forty per cent of *85* the people who said they didn't like the taste of kippers had never, in their entire lives, tasted kippers!

14   Finally, the marketers decided it is dangerous to assume that people can be trusted to behave in a rational way.

15   The Color Research Institute had what it felt was a startling *90* encounter with this proneness to irrationality when it tested package designs for a new detergent. It was testing to see if a woman is influenced more than she realises, in her opinion of a product, by the package. It gave the housewives three different boxes filled with detergent and requested that they try them all out for a few weeks *95* and then report which was the best for delicate clothing. The wives were given the impression that they had been given three different types of detergent. Actually only the boxes were different; the detergents inside were identical.

16   The design for one was predominantly yellow. The yellow in the *100* test was used because some merchandisers were convinced that yellow was the best colour for store shelves because it has very strong visual impact. Another box was predominantly blue without any yellow in it; and the third box was blue but with splashes of yellow.

17   In their reports the housewives stated that the detergent in the *105* brilliant yellow box was too strong; it even allegedly ruined their clothes in some cases. As for the detergent in the predominantly blue box, the wives complained in many cases that it left their clothes dirty looking. The third box, which contained what the institute felt was an ideal balance of colours in the package design, overwhelmingly *110* received favourable responses. The women used such words as 'fine' and 'wonderful' in describing the effect the detergent in that box had on their clothes.

18   A department store that had become sceptical of the rationality of

its customers tried an experiment. One of its slowest-moving items *115* was priced at fourteen cents. It changed the price to two for twenty-nine cents. Sales promptly increased thirty per cent when the item was offered at this 'bargain' price.

19   One of the most costly blunders in the history of merchandising was the Chrysler Corporation's assumption that people buy auto- *120* mobiles on a rational basis. It decided back in the early 1950s, on the basis of direct consumer surveys and the reasoning of its eminently sensible and engineering-minded executives, that people wanted a car in tune with the times, a car without frills that would be sturdy and easy to park. With streets and parking spaces becoming *125* increasingly packed with cars the times seemed obviously to call for a more compact car, a car with a shorter wheel base.

20   In 1953 *Tide*, a leading trade journal of marketing-management men, asked, 'Is This the End of the "Big Fat Car"?' and told of Chrysler's decision that such was the case, and its planned style *130* revolution for all its makes. The company's styling director was quoted as saying, 'The people no longer want to buy a big fat car. The public wants a slim car.' The article also mentioned that Chrysler had recently mailed stockholders a pamphlet entitled 'Leadership in Engines', an area where it felt it was supreme.   *135*

21   What happened? Chrysler's share of the auto market dropped from twenty-six per cent in 1952 to about thirteen per cent in 1954. The company was desperate. It looked more deeply into what sells cars and completely overhauled its styling. The result is shown in another article in *Tide* two years later. It reported: *140*

22   'Chrysler, going downhill in 1954, makes a marketing comeback. Whole line suffered mostly from styling. . . . . One look at this year's products tells the story. People want long, low cars today. So some of the new cars by Chrysler are as much as sixteen inches longer and three inches lower. Plymouth is now the longest car in the low- *145* price field. The Dodge is the first car with three-colour exteriors.'

23   The happy result (for Chrysler) was that its share of the market bounced back very substantially in 1955. *Tide* called it one of the most remarkable turnabouts in marketing history.

from *The Hidden Persuaders*

1 a What does the title suggest to you about:

  (i) the subject of the extract
  (ii) the author's attitude to his subject?

b What were the marketers' original three assumptions and why did they become suspicious of them?

c What is your view of:

  (i) the men who said they liked dry beer *(paragraph 6)*
  (ii) the housewives who preferred the blue and yellow package *(paragraphs 15–17)*
  (iii) the customers who paid twenty-nine cents for two items *(paragraph 18)*?

2 a The effectiveness of the passage partly depends on (i) **structure** and (ii) **illustration**. How would you demonstrate these points?

b **Jargon** and **specialised vocabulary** are terms we might apply to words and phrases associated with a particular topic. Find six such words or phrases in paragraphs 1–3.

c What is:

a 'confession magazine' *(line 48)* a 'sampling' *(line 82)* a 'client' *(line 82)* an 'executive' *(line 123)* a 'styling director' *(line 131)*?

d Here are the meanings of other words and phrases from the world of commerce and advertising, used by the author. Find the corresponding items, in paragraphs 13–22:

  (i) a company which designs and sells advertisements
  (ii) not selling very well
  (iii) questionnaires designed to get information about people's buying habits
  (iv) features with visual appeal rather than usefulness
  (v) a return to profitability.

e What words or phrases are **opposed** in meaning to:

  (i) 'the truth about their wants and dislikes' *(paragraph 7)*
  (ii) 'functional modern' *(paragraphs 10–11)*
  (iii) 'complained' *(paragraph 17)*?

f Many words carry a **value judgement**, often in addition to their basic meaning: thus 'murder' means more than 'kill'. An important word in this passage is 'rational', with related words 'rationality' and 'irrationality'.

 (i) Give the meaning of 'rational'.
 (ii) Explain the importance of this idea in the passage as a whole.
 (iii) Give examples from the passage of other words of this type (e.g. 'unpredictability' *(line 5)*, 'logical' *(line 20)*).

3 a   (i) From what you have gathered of the author's attitude and what you know of advertising, guess the topics dealt with in these later chapters of the book: 'Self Images for Everybody', 'Marketing Eight Hidden Needs', 'The Built-in Sexual Overtone', 'Class and Caste in the Salesroom', 'The Psycho-Seduction of Children'.
     (ii) Collect or invent advertisements illustrating these categories.

35 Package Tour
Sue Arnold

Sue Arnold took an Honours BA in English at Trinity College, Dublin. She worked as a journalist for *The Lancaster Evening News, The London Evening Standard, The Daily Sketch* and *The Tehran Journal*. She is perhaps best known for her articles in *The Observer*. She is married to a stockbroker and has three small daughters.

1 Half-way through lunch, a nine-foot man with distended jowls and muscles like dumbbells rippling beneath a green combat jacket came up to me and playfully boxed my ears. Regaining consciousness some while later, I asked the man next to me who my friendly assailant had been. 'The Incredible Hulk,' he said, barely looking up 5 from his roast potatoes. 'We're after the rights on him for sneakers.'
2   'Really?' I said, impressed. 'How fascinating. Maybe you should meet the gentleman on my left who wants to put Snoopy on black lead pencils.' The Snoopy man, who came from Stevenage, said dreamily that the sales target next year was 18,000 gross of black lead 10 Snoopy pencils, 35,000 gross in 1980, maybe half a million in five years . . . his voice broke.
3   There were 250 of us attending an extraordinary event in London called the Character Merchandising Conference. I can't remember why I went. I have been wary of cuddly cartoon characters ever since 15 a visit to California's Disneyland, when someone told me that Tinkerbell, a ravishing creature in spangled leotard who swung high above our heads from the Enchanted Castle to the Fairy Grotto on an aerial trapeze, was in fact a 76-year-old grandmother. As for merchandising, marketing and retailing, I know as much about these 20 as I do about the digestive system of the hermit crab. My mother wanted me to be a buyer for Dorothy Perkins, but I didn't pass the test.
4   But I *love* conferences. I love being referred to as a delegate and hearing announcements like, 'Will Mr Cyril Loveday of Chislehurst 25 Novelty Goods and Slipware please come to reception.' My last conference was a very serious affair in Cardiff called The International Convention on Humour and Laughter to which delegates from Swaziland and Samoa came armed with ethnic jokes and

154

passed resolutions about banana skins. No, you don't have to force 30
me to pin a name tag on my lapel, pick up a folder full of useless info
and say 'Look old chap, why don't we kick a few ideas about in the
bar?' I have attended conferences on ferret maintenance, heavy duty
floor coverings and scientology. And now I remember why I went to
the seminar on Character Merchandising. It was Mickey Mouse's 35
birthday that week. He was fifty.

5   I missed the first two speakers because I was waylaid by Uncle
Bulgaria at the door and then stopped off for a chat with the
Michelin Man. When I eventually penetrated the conference
chamber, a man in a dark suit was telling everyone how the point of 40
sales material of the Mr Men fruit lollipops had helped his company
to position the concept to a particular market segment. He talked in
an impassioned way about 'media exposure' and 'buzz words' and
the vital importance of lolly bag editorial content. Every now and
then words in huge block capitals like RELEVANCE flashed on to a 45
giant television screen next to the dais.

6   There followed a short cartoon film about a space age character
called Captain Kremmen who, among other things, wrestled with
Thargoids and Putrons. 'We are heading for an adventure that will
make "Gone With The Wind" look like a test card,' said the 50
narrator. A man called Sean advised us against using real personalities like footballers to promote goods because they might be
transferred or break a leg in the middle of a sales drive.

7   Finally an advertising executive told us a cautionary tale about
Tony the Kelloggs Frosties tiger. Not to be confused with the Esso 55
tiger – put a tiger in your tum, as opposed to your tank. Apparently,
after occupying 4.6 per cent of the national breakfast cereal market,
Frosties sales began to flag. Exhaustive research came up with the
fearful truth – Tony was overshadowing the Frosties. Instead of
clamouring for crispy sugar-coated corn, kids were clamouring for 60
tigers. An immediate counterthrust was launched. Tony was re-
assessed, given a new image, new jokes; Frosties sales soared.

8   In the foyer a delegate was saying, 'I hear Mr Topsy Turvy
yoghurt topped £1 $\frac{1}{4}$ million in retail sales last year,' in the same
solemn tones that a Prime Minister might use to announce a cabinet 65
reshuffle. Over lunch I discussed the viability of using Batman to
promote an industrial hand cleanser with a delegate from
Derbyshire. The cleanser is called Swarfega and he had a quarter of a
million to spend on promotion.

9   'Why are you here?' I asked a young Glaswegian.   70
      'I've got a package,' he said. 'A ready-made character called Robbie
the Robot, a film and a record, and I'm looking for a product to link it
to.'

'Gosh,' I said, 'What are the lyrics?' He sang them to me:

> 'I'll be your butler if you choose,   *75*
> I'll comb your hair and clean your
>   shoes
> Switch on to me,
> Your wish is my command.'

'Doesn't that limit your product a little to boot polish and vacuum *80* cleaners?' I asked. He gave me a withering look.

'Don't be so naïve darling. The Smurfs sell petrol don't they? Wise up.'

From The Observer magazine, 10 December, 1978

---

1 **a**   Say if and why you think this passage, in comparison with *The Trouble with People* (page 148), is

    (i) similar or dissimilar in aim
    (ii) more or less **formal** in style.

  b   (i) In what **context** might you normally expect to find: 'jowls' *(line 1)* 'dumbbells' *(line 2)* 'sneakers' *(line 6)* a 'trapeze' *(line 19)* 'editorial content' *(line 44),* a 'test card' *(line 50)* a 'cautionary tale' *(line 54)* 'lyrics' *(line 74)*?
    (ii) Choose two of the items and say what effect the writer achieves by introducing them into *this* context.

  c   (i) Who or what are:

    The Incredible Hulk, Snoopy, Disneyland, Tinkerbell, Chislehurst Novelty Goods and Slipware, Mickey Mouse, Uncle Bulgaria, The Michelin Man, Mr Men, Captain Kremen, Thargoids, Putrons, Tony, Mr Topsy Turvey, Swarfega, Robbie the Robot, The Smurfs? Say

    (ii) which of the items in the list are the odd ones out
    (iii) why the others form a group
    (iv) what the intelligent reader should do if he or she can't identify any item.

2 **a**   Explain the aptness of the title.

b The organisation of the article might be summed up as follows:

   (i) the happening – no introduction
   (ii) reminiscence
   (iii) relevant digressions
   (iv) conference people, paragraphs 1 to 8
   (v) dialogue as conclusion.

   Locate these stages in the article.

c Sue Arnold achieves a humorous effect in various ways, including the use of:

   (i) **jargon** (ii) **alliteration** (iii) **exaggeration** (iv) **colloquialisms** (v) **parody**.

   Into which of these categories would you put

   (i) 'useless info' *(line 31)*
   (ii) 'Regaining consciousness some while later' *(lines 3–4)*
   (iii) 'cuddly cartoon characters' *(line 15)*
   (iv) 'media exposure' *(line 43)*
   (v) 'An immediate counterthrust was launched' *(line 61)*?

d Find another example, in the article, of each of the categories mentioned in **c**.

e Some of the humour in the passage depends on **incongruity**, i.e. the sense that a given item is unexpected or out of place. Find three examples in paragraph 4.

3 Make up a dialogue

a between two 'promotion characters', or

b between a manufacturer of paper handkerchiefs and some competing 'package men', or

c between some children as they discover the 'character' inside a cereal packet.

36 Paradise

Laurie Lee

Laurie Lee is best known for the portrait of his Cotswold village childhood in
Cider with Rosie (1959), to which *As I Walked Out One Midsummer Morning*
(1969), describing his travels in Spain just before the Civil War, is a sequel. He
has also published poetry and essays.

1 It seems to me that the game of choosing one's Paradise is rarely a
rewarding pastime; it either produces images of vast banality, or
boredom on a cosmic scale: sometimes a kind of Killarney between
showers, ringing with Irish tenors, or a perpetual Butlin's rigged for
everlasting Bingo; for others an exclusive developed area in Stock 5
Exchange marble surrounded by cottonwool and celestial grass.
This last – perhaps the most popular and longest sold in the series –
has always had its own unimaginable horror, where, in the glaring
blue-white of the adman's heaven, the starched inmates have
nothing whatever to do except sit down, stand up, walk around the *10*
draughty halls, or hide behind the classical pillars.
2   Indeed, through the ages, man's various conceptions of Paradise
have seemed more often than not to teeter on the brink of hell. And
with the common element of eternity thrown in, there wouldn't be all
that much to choose between them – except that hell would seem to *15*
promise more entertainment.
3   Paradise, in the past, as a piece of Christian propaganda, never
really got off the ground. Too chaste, too disinfected, too much on its
best behaviour, it received little more than a dutiful nod from the
faithful. Hell, on the other hand, was always a good crowd-raiser, *20*
having ninety per cent of the action – high colours, high
temperatures, intricate devilries and always the most interesting
company available. In the eyes of priest, prophet, poet and painter,
Hades has always been a better bet than heaven. Milton's best-seller
was *Paradise Lost* (while *Paradise Regained* was just a plate of cold *25*
potatoes). The sulphurous visions of Savonarola, Danté and
Hieronymus Bosch are something by which we have always been
willingly and vigorously haunted. Of all the arts, only certain rare
passages of music seem ever to have touched the fringes of a credible
Paradise. *30*

4   The difficulty of trying to suggest in any detail what one's personal Paradise should be is like suddenly coming into enormous wealth. There are no limits or disciplines to contain one's grandiose plans, and the results are generally unfortunate.

5   Having said that, and declared some of the flaws in the game, the *35* time has come for me to outline my own banality. Paradise, for me, is a holding on to the familiar contained within some ideal scale of the past – an eighteenth-century thing, perhaps, in its grace and order (without its squalor and tribulations). I would have a landscape shelving gently between mountains to the sea, with pastures and *40* woods between them. There would be a small city on the coast, a couple of villages in the hills, and a hermitage hanging from one of the distant crags – a place of sonorous mystery, never to be visited, but from which oracles would be issued once a week. The city would be walled, terraced and luminescent, intimate and without wheeled *45* traffic. From its centre, the countryside would always be visible and could comfortably be reached on foot. Temperatures would be constant: 68° to 74° with no wind except a breeze from the sea. No rain either, except for unseen showers in the night, just enough to keep things green; or festive 'summer-rain days', known and *50* predictable, when a light warm mist would drift through the streets and gardens, and lovers would fasten their shutters and spend long whispering afternoons accompanied by the sound of moistures dripping from rose to rose.

6   Weather, in Paradise, would be varied, yet tactful, never attempt- *55* ing to achieve any monotonous perfection. There would also be long Nordic twilights for walks in the country, beside river or reeded lake, whose rustling waters, standing with tall grave birds, would reflect the sky's slow shade towards night. The pastoral landscape itself would be lightened by tall flowering grasses, bee-orchids, button *60* mushrooms and snails. Apart from songbirds, who would sing only at dawn and evening and the whisper of river and ocean – no noise: no explosion, public announcement, radio, hammering of buildings, motor-car, jetplane – only the deep, forgotten primeval silence which, like true darkness itself, is a natural balm of which man is now *65* almost totally deprived.

7   Breaking this silence, of course, there would have to be music, for any place without music is a hearth without fire; not music of brass, I think, but music of reed and strings whose sounds are the most potent ravishers of the senses. This music would be based in the skull, *70* to be switched on at will, and inaudible to others unless they wished to share it.

8   But what about people? Well mine would be a First Day Paradise, for a very solid reason. In it one would have no past, nor future, only

the new-peeled light of the present, and so put the unthinkableness of 75
eternity out of one's mind. The people of the city, fields and
mountains — wits, sages, children, lovers — would shine for you with
the original magic of first sight, as you yourself would shine for them.
Recognition, but no remembrance, would ensure that they were
members of a familiar society whom you could never accuse of 80
repeating themselves; while their pleasure in the newness of you
would spare you the purgatory of knowing that you might be boring
them. It might be agreeable to imagine that everyone grew im-
perceptibly younger, like Cary Grant in his old TV films, but having
no recollection, this wouldn't matter — each day would bring its fresh 85
confrontation, each love would be first and only.

9   Paradise would also restore some of the powers we lost in that long
descent from childhood to death.

10   Senses that failed would be returned to the keen, high level of their
beginnings. The child's animal sharpness of taste and smell — which 90
the adult knows only too well he's lost when he hears the adman
trying to prove he still has them — the ability to take in the whiff of
heat from summer grass in the morning, the oils in a leaf, the white
dust on a daisy, the different spirits in wood, in clay, in iron, all of
which allows the child to bind himself intimately to these objects, but 95
from which the adult is inexorably exiled. Paradise would bring back
these senses and the contacts they offer — the special aura of a house
as you open its door, a tang which tells you its history and the
character of all the people in it; the awareness of an invisible animal
close at hand in a wood; the girlish texture of a young calf's mouth: 100
and taste; the brutality of nursery medicines, the delight in a
common caramel, the sharp bitter milk of the dandelion root, the
acrid horse-breath of straw in a barn.

11   Surely, with the handing back of these powers, one might
reasonably ask also for the restoration of appetite. Sacred appetite, 105
so readily blunted on earth — at least, three parts of one's time to
denying it, whether it be for food or love, not for puritanical reasons
but in order to sharpen it to the edge when it could best celebrate the
thing it longed for.

12   But one needn't bother to ask what one would do in Paradise. 110
Timeless, without memory or sense of future, one would live out
each day new. An ideal landscape; mountains, fields and woods, and
the sea throwing up its light. A deep green silence outside the walls of
the city, or occasional sweet airs that delight and harm not; within
the city, companionship, the sibilant pleasure of bare feet on marble; 115
wine, oil, the smell of herbs, brown skin; oceans mirrored in eyes that
would be the only eternity.

160

13   Above all, I think I'd wish for one exclusive indulgence – the power to take off as one does in dreams, to rise and float soundlessly over the bright tiles of the city, over the oak groves and nibbling *120* sheep, to jostle with falcons on mountain crags and then sweep out over the purple sea.

14   On the rooftops, as I returned, silver storks, wings folded, would stand catching the evening light. There would be children in the patios playing with sleepy leopards, girls in the windows preparing *125* their lamps. Alighting on this terrace of heaven I would join my unjealous friends and choose one for the long cool twilight. Asking no more of the day than that I should be reminded of my body by some brief and passing pain; and perhaps be allowed one twinge of regret at the thought of the other world I'd lived in, a sense of loss *130* without which no Paradise is perfect.

From I Can't Stay Long

1   a   What are some of the 'flaws in the game' *(line 35)* which Laurie Lee considers in the first four paragraphs?

     b   (i) In paragraphs 1–7 *(lines 1–72)* the author mentions things he would include in or exclude from Paradise. Which of his choices do you agree with and which would you reverse?
          (ii) What other things would you want or not want in your own Paradise?

     c   Laurie Lee deals with the problem of boredom in Paradise in paragraphs 8 and 12. Give his solution and your comment on it.

     d   What sense experiences other than those mentioned would you want in Paradise?

     e   In Lee's Paradise there is no work, physical or mental, little pain or sorrow, no death. Make out a case for including one or more of these.

2   a   The essay contains a number of **allusions** which might cause difficulty to a foreign reader. Say how you would explain to a person from the Middle or Far East three of the following:

Butlin's *(line 4)* Bingo *(line 5)* Stock Exchange *(lines 5–6)* 'Christian propaganda' *(line 17)* Paradise Lost *(line 25)* Savonarola *(line 26)* Danté *(line 26)* Hieronymus Bosch *(line 28)* 'oracles' *(line 44)* Cary Grant *(line 84)*.

b Lee's essay could be described as romantic and poetic. What do these terms mean in this case?

c There are also touches of humour in the piece. Where are they, in your view?

3 a Decide which culture the foreign reader in **2a** belongs to, and after reading and discussion say what his/her picture of Paradise would be like.

b What is the difference between Paradise and Utopia?

c Which of the following ideas of Heaven and Hell seem to you most interesting?

(i) 'There is a land of pure delight
     Where saints immortal reign;
  Infinite day excludes the night,
     And pleasures banish pain.

  There everlasting spring abides,
     And never-withering flowers;
  Death, like a narrow sea, divides
     This heavenly land from ours.'

(Isaac Watts)

(ii) 'Heaven lies about us in our infancy.'

(William Wordsworth)

(iii) 'On the earth the broken arcs; in the heaven, a perfect round.'
(Robert Browning)

(iv) 'A Dungeon Horrible, on all sides round
  As one great Furnace flam'd, yet from those flames
  No light, but rather darkness visible
  Serv'd only to discover sights of woe,
  Regions of sorrow, doleful shades, where peace
  And rest can never dwell, hope never comes
  That comes to all; but torture without end

Still urges, and a fiery Deluge fed
With ever-burning Sulphur unconsum'd:
Such place Eternal Justice had prepar'd.'

(John Milton)

(v) 'Hell is a city much like London –
A populous and smoky city.'

(Percy B. Shelley)

(vi) 'Hell is other people.'

(Jean-Paul Sartre)

Glossary

(Within an entry, heavy type indicates a related word or cross-reference. The numbers in brackets refer to extracts where the questions following include the feature listed.)

abstract: non-physical; general; perceived in the mind. (30)

alliteration: repetition of a consonant sound, usually at the beginning of a word or syllable, e.g. 'So smooth, so sweet, so silv'ry is thy voice' (R. Herrick) (22, 35)

allusion: a reference, sometimes indirect, to a person, place, theory, etc. which the reader is assumed to have some knowledge of. A theologian might **allude** to Moses or Calvary; a scientist to Relativity. (2, 3, 7, 12, 15, 18, 26, 36)

analogy: a parallel case, with one or more points of resemblance. In some respects learning to write is **analogous** to learning to play chess. (1, 4, 24)

antithesis: the opposite of a point already made or understood, e.g. 'Prosperity doth best discover vice, but adversity doth best discover virtue' (F. Bacon) (22, 32)

assertion: a forceful statement, often controversial or unsupported by example, e.g. 'Patriotism is the last refuge of a scoundrel' (Dr Johnson) (4, 32)

assonance: repetition of a vowel sound, e.g. 'Pipe to the spirit ditties of no tone' (J. Keats) (22)

assumption: an idea or fact taken for granted. The writer may assume that the reader is familiar with certain data, or agrees with a certain opinion. (10)

balance: an arrangement of similar words or structures, often for rhetorical effect, e.g. 'The race is not to the swift, nor the battle to the strong' (*Proverbs*) (22)

bathos: anticlimax, intended or unintended, descending from the serious to the trivial, e.g.
'Here thou, great Anna! whom three realms obey,
Dost sometimes counsel take – and sometimes tea' (A. Pope) (10)

category: a set of similar items; a group or class. Thus words could be

164

categorised into 'content' words like 'father', 'eat', 'loyal'; and 'structural' words like 'which', 'and', 'although'. (6, 19, 24, 31)

cite: quote or refer to, often as an illustration. (12)

cohesion: the links between words, sentences and paragraphs. These **cohesive** links may be dependent on the grammatical structure or the relationship of ideas. (12)

colloquialism: word or phrase chiefly found in everyday speech, e.g. 'kids' (for children); 'I could have kicked myself.' (2, 35)

concede: to admit; to allow a point in an opposing argument. (5, 9)

concept: an idea or abstraction, usually of a general nature. The concept of justice is explored in *Measure for Measure*. (28, 30, 32)

concrete: physical; belonging to the world of sense experience. (30)

connotation: a meaning or **overtone** additional to the basic meaning or **denotation**. Thus for Christians, the words 'cross' and 'save' have acquired many important connotations. (3)

context: the words or sentences near a given word, phrase, etc.; the situation in which an item is found. (1, 3, 4, 11, 13, 17, 19, 35)

contradiction: a statement which denies or is inconsistent with a previous statement by the writer. (7, 12)

define: to give the meaning(s) of a word or phrase, sometimes with an explanation. Thus the **definition** of 'theatre' might be: 'A building with a stage on which plays are performed.' (11, 16, 27)

derivation: tracing the origin of a word from its roots. Thus 'motherly' derives from the Old English 'modor' and 'maternal' from the Latin 'mater'. (26)

emotive: appealing to the feelings rather than the intellect, e.g. 'We will get everything out of her (Germany) that you can squeeze out of a lemon and a bit more.' (Sir E. Geddes 1918) (9)

epithet: a descriptive word or phrase applied to a person, thing, etc. e.g. 'Scotland the brave'; 'that paragon of animals (man)' (Shakespeare) 'Hollow, empty, is the epithet justly bestowed on Fame' (G. Eliot) (7)

exaggeration: see **hyperbole**. (35)

example: an instance or point illustrating a general idea. For Mr Skimpole in *Bleak House* butterflies **exemplify** freedom:
'I only ask to be free. The butterflies are free. Mankind will surely not deny to Harold Skimpole what it concedes to the butterflies!' (C. Dickens) (5, 8, 12, 30, 31, 32)

explicit: openly stated; not **implied** or hinted at. (8, 19, 26)

formal/informal: as applied to language: serious, restricted or ceremonious, as opposed to everyday expressions, e.g. emoluments/pay; purchase/buy; 'He expired in indigent circumstances'/'He died poor'. (6, 10, 18, 22, 35)

frequency: the number of times a word occurs in a typical, large sample of English. 'Structure words' like 'the', 'and', 'on' are very common, but 'content words' vary between being common, e.g. 'father', 'black', 'eat', and rare, e.g. 'quince', 'eccentric', 'desiccate'. (30)

generalisation: a sweeping statement, often about life or experience, with or without supporting detail, e.g. 'It is a truth universally acknowledged, that a single man in possession of a good fortune must be in want of a wife.' (Jane Austen) (1, 8, 19, 30, 31)

hyperbole: **exaggeration**, e.g. 'She has more goodness in her little finger, than he has in his whole body.' (J. Swift) (18, 35)

hypothesis: a theory, often scientific or sociological, which needs further testing or evidence to prove its validity. e.g. 'Corporal punishment in schools has a damaging effect on the psychology of the child.' (16, 29)

illustration: an example used to support or explain an idea or argument, e.g. 'It's like a portmanteau – there are two meanings packed into one word' (L. Carroll) (1, 5, 28, 34)

imagery: figurative language, especially similes and metaphors, e.g.
'He doth bestride the narrow world
Like a Colossus, and we petty men
Walk under his huge legs.' (Shakespeare)
A single **image** may underlie a whole work, as in E. M. Forster's *A Passage to India* or D. Morris's *The Human Zoo* (15)

imperative: a 'command', often used for rhetorical effect, e.g. 'Go and catch a falling star' (Donne) (1)

implication: a point hinted at rather than given. A writer may **imply** what he does not state **explicitly**: his meaning may be **implicit**. (3, 4, 7, 10, 17, 19, 22, 23)

incongruity: something out of place or inappropriate. An **incongruous** remark is often humorous; as when Eliza Doolittle at a fashionable tea-party says, 'Not bloody likely!' (G. B. Shaw) (18, 35)

inference: a point or idea deduced from a passage of speech or writing, where it is not stated, merely implied. (6)

irony: words conveying a meaning different from the apparent meaning.

166

An **ironic tone** may produce a humorous or sarcastic effect, e.g. 'Brutus is an honourable man' (Shakespeare). (1, 6, 10, 18, 20)

jargon: the special vocabulary of a science, art, profession, etc. Thus in linguistics 'back-chaining' and 'interlanguage' are special terms while 'competence' and 'fossilisation' have special meanings. Sometimes jargon is criticised as when Hamlet mocks the lawyer's 'quiddities, quillities, tenures, recognizances' etc. (11, 34, 35)

juxtaposition: placing items close together, often for special effect, e.g. 'Only connect the prose and the passion, and both will be exalted.' (E. M. Forster) (10)

metaphor: an implied simile or comparison, e.g.
'Now is the winter of our discontent
Made glorious summer by this sun of York.' (Shakespeare)
Many idioms are **metaphorical**, e.g. 'the ghost of a smile'; 'in hot water'; 'breathing down my neck'. (1, 4, 5, 12, 15, 25)

oppostition: words, phrases or sentences in a passage placed so as to emphasise a contrast of idea, or **antithesis**. Dr Johnson opposes one idea of womanhood against another: 'A man is in general better pleased when he has a good dinner upon the table, than when his wife talks Greek.' (1, 7, 23, 31, 32, 34)

overtone: see **connotation**. (3)

paradox: an apparent contradiction, e.g. 'The child is father of the Man' (W. Wordsworth) (28)

paragraph: a section of written language, usually on one theme or incident, often consisting of a topic sentence plus supporting points. (24)

parody: a humorous imitation of a literary work or style. Lewis Carroll **parodied** a well known nursery rhyme:
'Twinkle, twinkle, little bat!
How I wonder what you're at. . . ' (35)

pun: a play on words: e.g. 'I wasted time, and now doth time waste me', (Shakespeare). 'That's the reason they're called lessons, the Gryphon remarked: because they lessen from day to day.' (Lewis Carroll) (18)

qualify: to add a point which alters a preceding idea or statement; to modify. Hamlet adds a **qualification** to his idea of death as a sleep which ends all troubles by adding:
'To sleep, perchance to dream, ay, there's the rub.' (5, 19, 27)

receptive/productive vocabulary: words, spoken or written, which we recognise but do not use/words we do use. The former considerably outnumber the latter. (16)

register: mode of expression in speech or writing, the choice of language being determined by the combination of speaker, situation and listener/reader. Thus a sermon would be in different register from a football commentary; a barrister would use a different register in court and at home. (9, 10)

rhetoric: the art of using language persuasively. **A rhetorical question** is a question used for emphasis to which the answer is obvious or unnecessary, e.g. 'Who would have thought the old man to have had so much blood in him?' (Shakespeare) (1, 6, 9)

simile: a comparison, used for illustration or effect, e.g.
'My Luve's like a red, red rose
That's newly sprung in June.' (Burns) (25)

slang: words and phrases peculiar to certain social groups. It is often colloquial, vivid, metaphorical and short lived, e. g. 'come the acid over' = exert authority; 'a sky-pilot' = a clergyman; 'a windbag' = a tedious talker. (11)

specialised vocabulary: words or phrases associated with a particular profession, activity, etc.; **technical terms**. (34)

structure: the arrangement or organisation of sentences, paragraphs or longer passages. (22, 34)

style: the manner in which a writer expresses himself. **Stylistic** features may include choice of words, sentence structure, figurative language etc. (9, 10)

summary: a statement of the main points of a passage, usually excluding illustrative detail; a précis. Its length may vary from a few sentences to a third or more of the length of the original. (9, 11, 24, 28, 30)

symbolic: standing for some other thing or idea. In T. S. Eliot's *Journey of the Magi* the 'three trees on the low sky' may suggest the Crucifixion. (19)

synonymous: similar in meaning to a given word. Note the **synonyms** in the line 'And the cities hostile and the towns unfriendly' (T. S. Eliot) (24)

syntax: the grammatical arrangement of words in a sentence. (22)

technical terms: terms from the special vocabulary of the arts, sciences, professions, sport, etc. (2, 16, 19)

thesis: an argument or line of thought running through a speech or passage. Darwin's *Origin of Species* develops the thesis of natural selection by the survival of the fittest. (18)

tone: the overall 'flavour' or character of a passage; the author's attitude as suggested by the style. (2, 7, 10, 13, 18)

understatement: saying less than the whole truth: e.g. 'She's not exactly the brightest in the family.' (10)

value judgment: a subjective view, an implied attitude or comment. Thus the word 'propaganda' conveys not only the basic meaning 'the spreading of ideas' but also usually a critical opinion of those ideas. (34)

Acknowledgements

The authors and publishers wish to thank the following for permission to reproduce printed matter:

page 1, Peter Laurie, *Staying Alive* (© Sunday Times); page 9, Ray Connolly, *John, Me and the Lancashire Treasure* (© Sunday Times); page 13, Gerald Leach, *Breeding Out Faults* from 'The Biocrats' (Jonathan Cape Ltd); page 16, David Lewis, *The Looking Glass Kids* from 'How to be a Gifted Parent' (Souvenir Press Ltd, £6.25); page 20, Mary Kenny, *Rebel Daughter* from 'Woman's Hour: a Selection'; page 24, Jill Tweedie, *The Tribe That Has Lost its Way* (The Observer); page 28, Margaret Mead, *Childhood Discipline* from 'Some Personal Views' (Angus & Robertson (UK) Ltd Publishers); page 32, Tony Jasper, from 'Understanding Pop' (SCM Press 1972), Louis Savary, from 'The Kingdom of the Downtown' (© 1967 by The Missionary Society of St. Paul the Apostle in the State of New York, Paulist Press); page 35, Willis Hall, *Child's Play* from 'Football Classified: An Anthology of Soccer' (Mitchell Beazley London Ltd); page 41, S K Weinberg and H Arond, *The Occupational Culture of the Boxer* from 'The Sociology of Sport' (by permission of the The University of Chicago Press, © 1952 by The University of Chicago); page 46, Alistair Maclean, *Life Really Starts When I Push That Button* from 'The Exciting World of Jackie Stewart' (Collins Publishers); page 54, Colin Leicester, *Life in the Year AD 2000* from 'New Horizons for Education' (Council for Educational Advance); page 58, Kenneth Allsop, *Notes on a War* from 'Scan' (A D Peters & Co Ltd); page 61, Lyall Watson, from 'Supernature' (© by Lyall Watson, Hodder & Stoughton Ltd); page 67, Malcolm Muggeridge, *Happiness* from 'Woman's Hour: a Selection' edited by Mollie Lee; page 70, Michael Osborne, *Seconds Out* (The Observer); page 74, J A Hadfield, 1954 (Pelican Books, 1954) pp. 65–67. (Reprinted by permission of Penguin Books Ltd); page 78, Ruth Harrison, *Their Time is Nearly Run Out* from 'Animal Machines' (Watkins Publishing House); pages 82–88, letters from The Scotsman; page 90, E S Turner, *Courting Customs* from 'A History of Courting' (Michael Joseph Ltd); page 95, Benjamin Spock, *The Sexes are Really Different* from 'Decent and Indecent'; page 100, Casey Miller and Kate Swift, *The Great Male Plot* from 'Words and Women' (Victor Gollancz Ltd); page 104, Trevor Fishlock, *Why Ms Is Cast Out* from 'The Times London Diary of 21 January 1981' (© The Times of London); page 105, Edwin Muir, *A Race of Thinking Animals?* from 'An Autobiography' (acknowledgement is made to Gavin Muir and the Hogarth Press); page 108, Geoffrey Robertson, *Death Wish Without Pride* (The Guardian); page 112, F R Barry, *Euthanasia* from 'Christian Ethics and Secular Society' (© by F R Barry 1966, Hodder and Stoughton Ltd); page 117, Richard Hoggart, *Changes in Working Class Life* from 'Speaking to Each Other' (Chatto & Windus Ltd); page 121, Frank Smith, *See Big Plane* from 'Reading' (Cambridge University Press); page 126, Walter Nash, *An Enormous Achievement* from 'Our Experience of Language' (B T Batsford Ltd); page 133, Desmond Morris, *Incidental Gestures* from 'Manwatching' (Jonathan Cape

Ltd); page 136, from 'Summerhill: A Radical Approach to Child Rearing' by A S Neill (© 1968 Hart Publishing Company); page 142, © 1974 by Claude Steiner, from 'Scripts People Live' (Grove Press Inc); page 148, Vance Packard, *The Trouble With People* from 'The Hidden Persuaders' (A P Watt Ltd); page 154, Sue Arnold, *Package Tour* (The Observer); page 158, Laurie Lee, *Paradise* from 'I Can't Stay Long' (André Deutsch Ltd, 1975).